Companion Study Guide

Matters of the Heart

Companion Study Guide

Matters of the Heart

Juanita Bynum

Charisma
HOUSE
A STRANG COMPANY

Most STRANG COMMUNICATIONS/CHARISMA HOUSE/SILOAM products are available at special quantity discounts for bulk purchase for sales promotions, premiums, fund-raising, and educational needs. For details, write Strang Communications/Charisma House/Siloam, 600 Rinehart Road, Lake Mary, Florida 32746, or telephone (407) 333-0600.

MATTERS OF THE HEART COMPANION STUDY GUIDE by Juanita Bynum
Published by Charisma House
A Strang Company
600 Rinehart Road
Lake Mary, Florida 32746
www.charismahouse.com

This book or parts thereof may not be reproduced in any form, stored in a retrieval system, or transmitted in any form by any means—electronic, mechanical, photocopy, recording, or otherwise—without prior written permission of the publisher, except as provided by United States of America copyright law.

Unless otherwise noted, all Scripture quotations are from the Amplified Bible: Old Testament © 1965, 1987 by the Zondervan Corporation; New Testament © 1954, 1958, 1987 by the Lockman Foundation. Used by permission.

Scripture quotations marked KJV are from the King James Version of the Bible.

Scripture quotations marked THE MESSAGE are from *The Message: The Bible in Contemporary English*, copyright © 1993, 1994, 1995, 1996, 2000, 2001, 2002. Used by permission of NavPress Publishing Group.

Scripture quotations marked NIV are from the Holy Bible, New International Version. Copyright © 1973, 1978, 1984, International Bible Society. Used by permission.

Cover design by Judith McKittrick
Interior design by Terry Clifton

Copyright © 2005 by Juanita Bynum
All rights reserved

Library of Congress Control Number: 2004103418
International Standard Book Number: 1-59185-471-7

05 06 07 08 09 — 987654321
Printed in the United States of America

CONTENTS

PREFACE

About This Book

THIS COMPANION STUDY guide has been designed to help you make the best use of my book *Matters of the Heart,* which, as of this writing, has been a bestseller for many months..

Whether you are a baby Christian or an "old" one, you can get something out of this book. It will give you a way to apply the truths that are laid out in *Matters of the Heart,* and it will be helpful to you whether or not you happen to have a copy of that book.

Did you know that you are designed for total happiness, absolute abundance, and complete peace? And did you know that such blessings are not just the special property of an elite group of holy people? God wants to give them to every believer.

Here is what you will find in each chapter of this study guide:

- Excerpts from the corresponding chapter in *Matters of the Heart,* to give you a framework
- Pertinent scriptures, including a special one for each chapter that you might want to memorize
- Exercises of various types to help you think through and apply the ideas (You can write in this book.)
- A thought-provoking personal testimony
- "Heartbeat"—a brief summary of the main point of each chapter
- A prayer that you can personalize

The chapters of this study guide match the chapters of *Matters of the Heart,* plus this preface and a wrap-up chapter. You may decide to work through a chapter a week, which would take you about three months, or you may accomplish it more quickly. The chapters are designed to build on each other, but if you have already read *Matters of the Heart* and find that you would like some in-depth application help with particular concepts, you might decide to skip directly to the chapter in which you are the most interested.

You can use this book in discussion groups or all by yourself. (If you do use it alone, see if you can share what you are learning with at least one other friend. It always helps to talk about spiritual growth.)

MOVING TOWARD A NEW HEART

As we move through this book together, you will learn to:

- Listen to the new heart (God's gift to you, if you ask!).
- Renew your mind daily.
- Get a *relationship* going with God.
- Please Him in everything!

When the renewed mind lines up with the conversion that is in your heart, you are a new creature—completely—inside and out. I want to help you get a new heart and a renewed mind.

INTRODUCTION

How It All Began

IT WAS DIFFICULT for me to receive this message about a new heart. I already had a major "platform" and was in the public eye. But that did not matter to God. Though it was painful and slow, I had to begin taking that deep, inner look. Like so many others, I wanted to concentrate my efforts on my overt walk with the Lord, where I was more interested in what others thought of me than I was with what God thought about me.

As God began to deal with me, He started showing me that my "burden" was not for the people to whom I ministered. I was more concerned for my image, what I would project to others. The Lord exposed my true situation to me, saying, "Jesus made Himself of no reputation, yet it is your reputation that has become most important to you. You are thinking about all that you are doing, the major platforms where you are able to speak and all the exposure that you are getting. But what is the condition of your heart toward Me and toward My people?"

He continued, "Let Me show you some little things…." And He started surfacing things about my personality, things I had reasoned were "just me," but really, they were errors in my heart. He said, "The sad thing is, you are so far away from Me. You are nowhere near Me, though you think that you are."

Then He said, "I want to give you a new heart."

I was not expecting to receive a "new heart" message. I felt that I had given my heart to God when I was converted. But somewhere along the way it had gone into a dormant state. I had begun to operate from my "works," not from my heart.

I knew that I had accepted Christ as my personal Savior. My heart had been converted, and I began to get into the Word. Then somewhere along the line I started reading the Word of God to prepare me to preach the gospel—not to convert my own mind. And even though I was preaching a powerful gospel, I was having difficulties and struggles in my personal life. My ministry had become my career. I realized that my heart was sick (Jer. 17: 9–10).

The heart is deceitful above all things, and it is exceedingly perverse and corrupt and severely, mortally sick! Who can know it [perceive, understand, be acquainted with his own heart and mind]? I the Lord search the mind, I try the heart, even to give to every man according to his ways, according to the fruit of his doings.

—JEREMIAH 17:9–10

God had tried my heart, and I had failed the test. I was doing a religious work, and still I was backslidden in my heart. I did this without realizing it, because of the wonderful responses of people to my works. I even felt God's anointing and presence upon my works. But I never stopped to recheck my heart to see if it was in right standing with God.

I had to be honest with myself and realize that my heart was not right. I had to ask myself, "Am I sure, beyond the shadow of a doubt, that Jesus lives in me? I do not have any doubt that He uses me, but does Jesus live here? Am I His?"

It was as if I experienced an awakening. God convicted me.

WE MUST RECEIVE THE NEW HEART

Like King David, I cried out to God, "Create in me a clean heart, O God, and renew a right, persevering, and steadfast spirit within me" (Ps. 51:10).

He did it! He gave me a new heart! I was renewed. I became a new person. Brand-new.

> *Create in me a clean heart, O God, and renew a right, persevering, and steadfast spirit within me.*
>
> —PSALM 51:10

Since that time, I have also been compelled to give others the same opportunity. God has birthed a "new heart" message in me!

The most important thing is to have the new heart—and to know that you have it. We must all come to a place where we either admit that we do not have a new heart or that we have mastered the act of salvation and become the great pretenders. What has happened to the church across the board is that we have become men pleasers. We have taught each other to master the church "act." Everybody looks saved; we know how to act saved; we know how to do saved stuff; and we know how to project a "saved" image to others. But our hearts are far from it—we are not even close.

We are the great pretenders. To all who fit into that category, one day Jesus will say, "You say you have cast out devils in My name and have healed the sick in My name—but begone from Me; I never knew you." (See Matthew 25:41.) Don't let Him say that to you! What Jesus means is this: "I never had a relationship with YOU. You worked for Me, but I did not have a relationship with you."

The "new heart" was Jesus' greatest message. It is the Bible's greatest story. In all of Scripture, that with which God is most concerned is this vital truth—the matters of the heart.

Are You Saved?

As you have therefore received Christ, [even] Jesus the Lord, [so] walk (regulate your lives and conduct yourselves) in union with and conformity to Him. Have the roots [of your being] firmly and deeply planted [in Him, fixed and founded in Him], being continually built up in Him, becoming more confirmed and established in the faith, just as you were taught, and abounding and overflowing in it with thanksgiving.
—COLOSSIANS 2:6–7

1.   How did you begin your life in Christ? How would you describe it to someone?

_____

_____

_____

2.   Do you feel you have continued to be "built up in Him, becoming more confirmed and established in the faith, just as you were taught"? Why or why not?

_____

_____

_____

3.   Circle your answer: Would you describe your heart as a thankful one?

   a. almost never
   b. once in a while
   c. pretty often
   d. most of the time
   e. always, every minute of the day or night

4.   Do your answers indicate to you a course of action? If so, write out your resolve.

   I, [name] _____, resolve to do the following:

_____

_____

Heart to Heart

From your heart, write a simple prayer to God. It will touch His heart. You could write something like this:

Dear God,

I want to understand more about the new heart You want to give me. I am beginning to become aware of problems within myself. Here is a partial list of some of my symptoms of "heart trouble":

_____

_____

_____

Please give me the grace to seek You until I am sure I have received a new heart. Thank You, and amen.

 H E A R T ᴮ E A T H E A R T ᴮ E A T H E A R T ᴮ E A T

Our hearts are sick, and they mislead us.
God wants to give us new, healthy hearts.

CHAPTER 1

We Need a New Heart

WE ARE ALL struggling in our own way, trying to make sure that we "do right" from our hearts. We become experts at keeping up appearances, and most of us deceive ourselves into thinking that we are succeeding in becoming righteous. But the truth is that no amount of struggling and effort can produce results good enough to please God.

As I began to question God about this new heart, I started to observe people in ministry. I looked at the church. I saw the choirs dressed in beautiful robes and the praise and worship teams with their matching outfits. One pastor would have on a nice, Versace suit and tie, and his wife would be sitting there with a St. John knit on—it all looked so perfect. It oozed "spiritual perfection"—to the point that it became a problem for me.

The more I looked at the problem, the more I was forced to turn around and look within myself at my own situation. "OK, Juanita," I said to myself, "what is your problem? What is it that bothers you about this so-called walk with the Lord?"

I realized that through the years my problem had been my own feelings of spiritual inadequacy. I would look at my spiritual superiors and think to myself, *I can never become that.* I could never be like the many people that God had placed in my life as spiritual examples. I felt that I could never be like them because they were the epitome of spiritual perfection. Their status, to me, was unattainable. At the same time, in other people's eyes my own image had become unattainable, too. None of it was reality.

If we consistently paint a picture that everything is perfect, beautiful, and wonderful—"You know you have reached God when you look like me...dress like me...walk and talk like me"—then we have totally missed God! We have become a group of people who constantly pursue an image—not God!

What does God require of us? Do we understand that our life in the church is founded on an individual relationship that each one of us must have with the Lord alone?

A new heart will I give you and a new spirit will I put within you, and I will take away the stony heart out of your flesh and give you a heart of flesh. And I will put my Spirit within you and cause you to walk in My statutes, and you shall heed My ordinances and do them. And you shall dwell in the land that I gave your fathers; and you shall be My people, and I will be your God. I will also save you from all your uncleannesses.

—Ezekiel 36:26–29

THE BRAIN HAS ASSUMED CONTROL

This world has become a brain world. Our activities are directed by our finite brains. Our lives are constructed and instructed by the laws of our intellects. The brain teaches us how to scheme, lie, connive, and manipulate.

And yet, God has put a spirit of conviction in our hearts, which corrects us when we do something wrong. The world around us is busy training us to bypass the conviction of our heart. No one is seeking after God for a changed, new heart. We do not want to change; we only want to feel better—for the moment.

Everybody is moved by their emotions through their logical

Spiritual Inadequacy

1. Do you feel outclassed or even intimidated spiritually by someone else?

_____

_____

2. If you have been plagued with feelings of spiritual inadequacy that cause you to think that you can never be as good as your "spiritual superiors," have you tried to compensate for such feelings by working harder on the image you project to others?

_____

_____

3. What part of the image you project to others is the most important to you (for example, your physical appearance, a particular personality trait, your giftedness, your "cool")? Think about what you may have in mind when you "glance over your shoulder" to impress someone.

_____

_____

minds, which always look out for "Number One." Emotions and logic react to the "threats" they perceive around them—everybody else is always wrong. This is how the "old heart" rules.

Every way of a man is right in his own eyes, but the Lord weighs and tries the heart. . . . Haughtiness of eyes and a proud heart, even the tillage of the wicked or the lamp [of joy] to them [whatever it may be], are sin [in the eyes of God].

—PROVERBS 21:2–4

Getting Personal

I have been a Christian for most of my adult life. When I was in my twenties, God delivered me from alcohol and gave me a good church. I knew Jesus as my Savior, but I had no idea that He could do more than He had already done. I read my Bible and was no longer living in sin. I had forgiven the people who had done me wrong. But I had no power against the darkness within my heart. Like a lot of people, I thought that if I felt like I was a victim of circumstances, I was not guilty of anything. But I couldn't really change my circumstances. So how would I ever change the darkness in my heart? I was restless and tense. No one had ever told me that Jesus could awaken your spirit and make your heart one with His. I just had no idea how much more He wanted to be available to every believer.

—*D. W.*

WHAT DOES THE BIBLE
SAY ABOUT IT?

The Bible says that we are born in sin and shaped in iniquity. (See Psalm 51:5.) We are born with an "old heart" nature that is already coated with the potential to do wrong. When we come into the world, our hearts are already shaped for sin.

Iniquity is anything you do that God is not in. It is anything done against the will of God or against the laws or nature of God. If something is contrary to His character, it is iniquity. Short of getting a heart transplant, we are stuck with this old, iniquitous heart.

In other words, we are training to become professional sinners.

When we look at our society, we see that this is true—and I am not just talking about the secular world; I am talking about the church! We are in church, dancing and shouting and speaking in tongues, yet we have hearts of iniquity just like the world. We have built houses, and we have multiplied our strength. Our silver has been multiplied, our gold has been multiplied, and now our minds and our hearts are lifted up—against God and against each other—full of pride. We have forgotten the Lord.

When we walk with our old hearts that are shaped in iniquity, hearts that are born into sin, seeking the Lord is not important. This old heart does not come with a "Yes, Lord" in it.

Deuteronomy 10:12 says that there is no way to walk in the ways of God unless you fear the Lord and love Him "with all thy heart and with all thy soul" (KJV). *Strong's Concordance* tells us that the word *soul* indicates all of our mind and all of our emotions. We cannot walk in His ways unless we submit our mind and emotions to Him and love Him from the center of our being, our heart.

Can our old heart, which was "born in sin and shaped in iniquity," love God? The only way that we can truly love God is to love

---

Old Heart Test

Proverbs 6:16–19 lists seven characteristics of our old hearts. How many of these can you personally identify with?

- ☐ "A proud look" ("looking down your nose" at anyone)

- ☐ "A lying tongue" (telling lies, big or little ones)

- ☐ "Hands that shed innocent blood" (killing someone, including abortion, and including wanting to murder someone—see Matthew 5:21–22)

- ☐ Manufacturing "wicked thoughts and plans" (plotting mischief or illegal acts)

- ☐ Being "swift in running to evil" (thoughtlessly plunging into action, motivated by anger, selfishness, or peer pressure)

- ☐ Being "a false witness who breathes out lies" (misrepresenting the facts of a situation for your personal benefit)

- ☐ Being a person "who sows discord" (starting arguments)

If you are a human being (and if you are honest), you will have made check marks! This helps prove how much we need a new heart from God.

Him with the same love that He has given to us. It comes from Him so we can give it back to Him. And He can't put His love into old hearts. That would be like putting new wine into old wineskins. (See Matthew 9:16–17.)

And now, Israel, what does the Lord your God require of you but [reverently] to fear the Lord your God, [that is] to walk in all His ways and to love Him, and to serve the Lord your God with all your [mind and] heart and with your entire being. To keep the commandments of the Lord and His statutes which I command you today for your good?

—DEUTERONOMY 10:12–13

ASK FOR A NEW HEART

We, God's people, must ask for a new heart. Are we willing to do this? We have to plow deeply into the church system to find people who are crying to God, a remnant sitting in the body of Christ in this hour that is willing to say, "I have to have the heart of God. I have to have a new heart. I have to be able to have a real relationship with God outside of the pews, outside of the choir roll, outside of my favorite preacher or evangelist. How do I get back to God—simply God?" Simply God, without all the props. Simply God, without all the drama.

Church and a past record of sincere prayers and resistance of sin are not enough—we must live in a relationship that will *keep us on track.*

God wants to provoke His people unto righteousness. He doesn't want us to be complacent. He wants us to ask for a new heart.

Ask Yourself...

Do I live by a "gospel of the church," or do I live by the gospel of God's love?

1.   Describe one way in which you may have lived as if the church structure or expectations were more important than God.

_____

_____

_____

2.   Have you obtained some benefits or rewards for doing this?

_____

What kinds of benefits?

_____

_____

3.   Do you feel God wants you to make some adjustments?

_____

> *And you shall [earnestly] remember all the way which the Lord your God led you these forty years in the wilderness, to humble you and to prove you, to know what was in your [mind and] heart, whether you would keep His commandments or not.*
>
> —DEUTERONOMY 8:2

JESUS' HARD SAYINGS

Jesus said, "If anyone loves me, he will obey my teaching.... He who does not love me will not obey my teaching" (John 14:23–24, NIV). This statement is hard to deal with, especially in view of Jesus' "hard sayings."

DO

1. Reconcile with people you have wronged (Matt. 5:23–24)

2. Love your enemies (Matt. 5:43–47)

3. Keep your promises (Matt. 5:33)

4. Be generous to everybody (Matt. 5:40–42)

5. Love and pray for your enemies (Matt. 5:44)

6. Be perfect (Matt. 5:48)

7. Forgive everybody (Matt. 6:12, 14)

8. Fast (Matt. 6:16–18)

9. Accumulate spiritual treasure (Matt. 6:20–21)

10. Seek righteousness (Matt. 6:33)

DON'T

1. Commit murder (Matt. 5:21)

2. Angrily insult someone (Matt. 5:22)

3. Commit adultery (Matt. 5:27)

4. Look lustfully on someone (Matt. 5:28–29)

5. Get a divorce (Matt. 5:32)

6. Take vengeance (Matt. 5:39–40)

7. Show off (Matt. 6:1–8, 16–18)

8. Accumulate riches or love money (Matt. 6:19, 24)

9. Worry (Matt. 6:25–34)

10. Judge others (Matt. 7:1–2)

For a review of some of Jesus' hard-to-obey teachings, take your Bible and read His Sermon on the Mount in chapters 5, 6, and 7 of Matthew. On page 14 is a summary of His commands from these chapters. Circle those that give you the most trouble and, in the extra space below each answer, elaborate briefly as to why you find the circled commands hard to obey.

Is it humanly possible to obey all of these commands?

- The answer is easy—NO!

Then why does Jesus say that we prove our love for Him by obeying such impossible demands? Is He trying to make it impossible for us to be saved?

- WE HOPE NOT!

Why are His standards so high? Is He trying to provoke us to do something?

- YES!

What if we found Someone who would be a perfect "stand in" for us?

- WE *DO* HAVE SOMEONE!

Let's let Him be our substitute by saying, "I'm trading in my old heart for a new one that can connect with You." We will never be able to get an "A+" in obedience unless we ask Him to stand in for us. As we connect with Him (using our new hearts), we *will* be able to love and please God.

> Now may the God of peace [Who is the Author and the Giver of peace], Who brought again from among the dead our Lord Jesus, that great Shepherd of the sheep, by the blood [that sealed, ratified] the everlasting

agreement (covenant, testament), strengthen (complete, perfect) and make you what you ought to be and equip you with everything good that you may carry out His will; [while He Himself] works in you and accomplishes that which is pleasing in His sight, through Jesus Christ (the Messiah); to Whom be the glory forever and ever (to the ages of the ages). Amen (so be it).

—HEBREWS 13:20–21

"CHURCH" IS NOT ENOUGH

I look at Solomon's example and am concerned about the longevity of the church. If we, the church, do not make this switch—the switch from being a religious organization to having a relationship with our Father—then we are going to fail in our efforts. We will not be able to accomplish what God has given us to do.

King Solomon inherited the kingdom of his father, David. Yet in 1 Kings 11:3, we discover that "his wives turned away his heart from God." Even though he began his reign over Israel by seeking God's wisdom, and even though he built the temple of God, his kingdom became little more than a religious organization—and he lost his relationship with his Father God. He followed his foreign-born wives into the worship of false gods, building temples of worship to their idols (v. 8). As a result, "the Lord was angry with Solomon because his heart was turned from the Lord, the God of Israel" (v. 9).

Just as it was with Solomon, I believe God's anger is kindled against us when He sees us turn from Him and begin walking in the way of the world around us. Like Solomon, we do not even realize that our hearts are being drawn away. We may even say, "I've been religious all my life. Do I really need a new heart? Why would God be angry with me?" We may have walked closely with God in the past and, like Solomon, may have even prayed for His wisdom to guide our steps. God had already appeared to Solomon and commanded him that he should not go after other gods (v. 9). However, Solomon did not do what the Lord had commanded. His disobedience kindled the anger of God.

Like Solomon, many believers have prosperity in their own eyes. They—perhaps I should say "we"—have built mighty temples to God, just as Solomon did. We in the church have considered ourselves to be "structured" and "mighty." We think that we have all of the answers. We have an appearance of God. We have received the accolades of men. But it is at this very point of success that the heart can be in its greatest form of deception.

> *The heart is deceitful above all things, and it is exceedingly perverse and corrupt and severely, mortally sick! Who can know it [perceive, understand, be acquainted with his own heart and mind]?*
>
> —JEREMIAH 17:9

We need a new heart, because the one we were born with is "deceitful above all things."

Hear me. It is time to seek God like never before. It is time to fall down at the altar and ask Him to renew your heart. It is time to become more like Jesus, for real! "Church as usual" is over! It is time to take off the "old wineskin" and put on the "new man."

> Keep on asking and it will be given you; keep on seeking and you will find; keep on knocking [reverently] and [the door] will be opened to you.
>
> —MATTHEW 7:7–8

Memory Verse	*Create in me a clean heart, O God, and renew a right, persevering, and steadfast spirit within me.*
	—PSALM 51:10

Heart to Heart

O God, my old heart is causing me to behave in ways that don't please You. Specifically, I have the most trouble with [inadequacy, resentment, irritation, etc.]:

_____

_____

_____

I am not happy about these things. I want to change, but I need Your help so I can carry through with the changes.

Please make me able to desire You more than anything else in the world.

In Jesus' name, amen.

HEARTBEATHEARTBEATHEARTBEAT

Each of us needs to ask God for a new heart. The heart we were born with leads us astray.

CHAPTER 2

We Have an Inside-Out Problem

WE WOULD PREFER to blame "outside forces" for the mess we are in. It's so easy for us to say, "Well, I am evil because this or that happened to me."

Jesus teaches us:

> Do you not discern and see that whatever goes into a man from the outside cannot make him unhallowed or unclean....What comes out of a man is what makes a man unclean and renders [him] unhallowed. For from within, [that is] out of the hearts of men, come base and wicked thoughts, sexual immorality, stealing, murder, adultery, coveting (a greedy desire to have more wealth), dangerous and destructive wickedness, deceit; unrestrained (indecent) conduct; an evil eye (envy), slander (evil speaking, malicious misrepresentation, abusiveness), pride (the sin of a heart uplifted against God and man), foolishness (folly, lack of sense, recklessness, thoughtlessness). All these evil [purposes and desires] come from within, and they make the man unclean and render him unhallowed.
>
> —MARK 7:18, 20–23

The problem is not what is entering your life from external sources. It is not the fault of what is taking place around you. Those things that come "at you" from external sources are merely identifying with something that is already in your heart. Instead of pretending to be holy on the outside, we should focus on what is inside. If

Getting Personal

It's faulty thinking to assume that because you are able to keep up with a list of spiritual activities, your heart has become new. I used to be convinced that I was doing everything I was supposed to do: attending church weekly, attending retreats and special events at my church, raising my children to believe in Jesus, giving 10 percent of my money to the offering. I knew that I was doing more than the average person. I was even memorizing passages from the Bible and taking notes during the pastor's sermons. But I was so intense about my life. Finally I realized that God looks only on my heart, not at my efforts. Never mind I was trying to live the way Jesus taught us to live—I was missing the main point, which is how He wants us to do everything, through Him, in relationship with Him, letting Him work through my new heart.

—*B. G.*

we ask God to give us a new heart, this heart will begin to manifest on the outer man just as the old heart works from the inside out.

WHAT IS OUR OLD HEART LIKE?

We can begin to understand the condition of our old heart by taking a closer look at Jeremiah 17:9: "The heart is *deceitful* above all things, and it is exceedingly *perverse* and corrupt and *severely, mortally sick*" (emphasis added).

"*Deceitful.*" In this verse the word *deceitful* means "to mislead by a false appearance or statement; to trick." God calls the old heart "deceitful above all things." It does not matter how much you try, how many Bible studies you attend, or how many times you go to church. No, this wicked heart not only misleads people, but it also misleads *you*. This heart gives a false appearance, not just to people, but also to *you*. It makes you think, *Because I look right, I am right.*

But there is another definition for the word *deceitful*. It also means "to be unfaithful." This heart is unfaithful. It can never be dedicated to God. It can never keep a commitment. This deceitful heart does not have what it takes to be faithful to anything—God or man.

"Perverse." The word *perverse* means that this heart is "willfully determined not to do what is expected or desired." It is "turned away from what is right, good, or proper." This heart has a willful desire built in. This is why, even when we teach from the Word of God (expecting that, as a result, people will follow our teaching), they do not walk in the light of truth. We expect them to be different, but if the heart within them is like the heart described in Jeremiah 17, it comes with a built-in will that says, "I will not yield to God. I will not obey the things of God." Rebellion is part of the makeup of the old heart.

"Severely, mortally sick." Our old heart is not just mortally sick, but it is severely, mortally sick. This heart destroys everything that it touches. It can act "seemingly" for a little while, but this heart eventually tears up relationships. It is harsh, not kind. This heart is *mortally* sick, which means that it will lead you to your grave. It will literally steal your life away.

What Does the Heart Do?

The "heart" is at the heart of the Bible. More often than any other topic, the "heart" is addressed in both the Old and New Testaments. (Most of the other topics are actually matters of the heart. For instance, *emotions* are matters of the heart. *Obedience* is a matter of the heart. *Worship* is a matter of the heart.)

Any heart, old or new, has the same types of functions—for evil or for good. Read the verses below. Then match the verse to the *function* of the heart that the verse illustrates. The first one is done as an example.

1.   "But Mary was keeping within herself all these things (sayings), weighing and pondering them in her heart" (Luke 2:19).

2.   "Therefore also now, says the Lord, turn and keep on coming to Me with all your heart, with fasting, with weeping and with mourning [until every hindrance is removed and the broken fellowship is restored]. Rend your hearts and not your garments and return to the Lord, your God" (Joel 2:12–13).

3.   "Let each one [give] as he has made up his own mind and purposed in his heart" (2 Cor. 9:7).

4.   "My heart was hot within me. While I was musing, the fire burned" (Ps. 39:3).

5.   "My heart trusts in, relies on, and confidently leans on Him, and I am helped" (Ps. 28:7).

6.   "Love one another fervently from a pure heart" (1 Pet. 1:22).

7.   "A calm and undisturbed mind and heart are the life and health of the body, but envy, jealousy, and wrath are like rottenness of the bones" (Prov. 14:30).

8.   "Speak out to one another in psalms and hymns and spiritual songs, offering praise with voices [and instruments] and making melody with all your heart to the Lord, at all times and for everything giving thanks in the name of our Lord Jesus Christ to God the Father" (Eph. 5:19–20).

9.   "When Saul saw the Philistine host, he was afraid; his heart trembled greatly" (1 Sam. 28:5).

10.   "You have put more joy and rejoicing in my heart than [they know] when their wheat and new wine have yielded abundantly" (Ps. 4:7).

11.   "Only take heed, and guard your life diligently, lest you forget the things which your eyes have seen and lest they depart from your [mind and] heart all the days of your life" (Deut. 4:9).

12.   "But Hezekiah did not make return [to the Lord] according to the benefit done to him, for his heart became proud" (2 Chron. 32:25).

13.   "For out of the heart come evil thoughts (reasonings and disputings and designs) such as murder, adultery, sexual vice, theft, false witnessing, slander, and irreverent speech" (Matt. 15:19).

14.   "For when Solomon was old, his wives turned away his heart after other gods, and his heart was not perfect (complete and whole) with the Lord his God" (1 Kings 11:4).

15.   "I have inclined my heart to perform Your statutes forever, even to the end" (Ps. 119:112).

16.   "Peter said, Ananias, why has Satan filled your heart that you should lie to and attempt to deceive the Holy Spirit, and should [in violation of your promise] withdraw secretly and appropriate to your own use part of the price from the sale of the land?" (Acts 5:3).

17.   "And you shall love the Lord your God with all your [mind and] heart and with your entire being and with all your might" (Deut. 6:5).

18.   "You shall not hate your brother in your heart" (Lev. 19:17).

19.   "And I will give them a heart to know (recognize, understand, and be acquainted with) Me, that I am the Lord; and they will be My people, and I will be their God, for they will return to Me with their whole heart" (Jer. 24:7).

20.   "For with the heart a person believes (adheres to, trusts in, and relies on Christ) and so is justified (declared righteous, acceptable to God)" (Rom. 10:10).

16	Lying	____	Loving people
____	Feeling peace	____	Loving God
____	Worshiping God	____	Believing
____	Worshiping idols	____	Hating
____	Remembering	____	Being generous
____	Feeling fear	____	Deep thinking
____	Being proud	____	Repenting
____	Feeling anger	____	Obeying God
____	Feeling joy	____	Doing evil
____	Knowing God	____	Trusting God

Can you think of other functions of the heart?

_____

_____

_____

_____

_____

THE INSENSITIVE HEART OF MAN

Jesus also said, quoting the prophet Isaiah:

> For this nation's heart has grown gross (fat and dull), and
> their ears heavy and difficult of hearing, and their eyes
> they have tightly closed, lest they see and perceive with
> their eyes, and hear and comprehend the sense with their
> ears, and grasp and understand with their heart, and turn
> and I should heal them.
>
> —MATTHEW 13:15

The apostle Paul adds:

> Their moral understanding is darkened and their rea-
> soning is beclouded. [They are] alienated (estranged,
> self-banished) from the life of God [with no share in it;
> this is] because of the ignorance (the want of knowledge
> and perception, the willful blindness) that is deep-seated
> in them, due to their hardness of heart [to the insensitive-
> ness of their moral nature].
>
> —EPHESIANS 4:18

Do you see it? People who operate from their soulish realm,
through their minds, are incapable of producing anything of eternal
value.

Self Test

Finish these sentences by describing what you do in these circumstances:

• When I am worried, I cope by...

_____

• When I am angry, I tend to...

_____

• When I am overwhelmed, I want to...

_____

• When I am joyful, I like to...

_____

• When I want to relax, I prefer to...

_____

Do your actions seem to line up with biblical standards?

_____

Do your answers point to a renewed heart or an old heart?

_____

(They might be mixed, and that's fine. You might be growing into your new heart.)

THORNY OR ROCKY SOIL?

How is the evil one able to snatch a Word that has been sown in someone's heart? He is familiar with the grounds—they are legally his. Satan already knows the base character of that heart, and he knows that it does not have what it takes to absorb and hold that Word.

Listen then to the [meaning of the] parable of the sower: While anyone is hearing the Word of the kingdom and does not grasp and comprehend it, the evil one comes and snatches away what was sown in his heart....As for what was sown on thin (rocky) soil, this is he who hears the Word and at once welcomes and accepts it with joy; yet it has no real root in him, but is temporary (inconstant, lasts but a little while); and when affliction or trouble or persecution comes on account of the Word, at once he is caused to stumble [he is repelled and begins to distrust and desert Him Whom he ought to trust and obey] and he falls away.

—Matthew 13:18–21

When the Word of the Lord tries to penetrate into that heart, it cannot, because holy things are illegally trespassing on the enemy's ground. The earth realm is legal ground for Satan. He is "the prince of the power of the air" (Eph. 2:2). The worldly realm is his, but he has not been given authority over the spiritual realm. This is why believers must walk in the Spirit.

Are you getting the revelation? God warns that if you do not walk in the Spirit (and the way to "walk" in the Spirit is to receive the "new heart" of the Spirit), then Satan can take anything righteous that hits those grounds. He has a legal right to cancel it! You have given the right to him.

Emotionalism. Many people hear the Word and "accept it with joy." You can see it every Sunday in the church. People holler back at the preacher, shouting, "Amen, preach it!" Too often these are the ones who hear the Word, but without real heart penetration. There is no depth so the Word can't take root. It floats around in the emotional realm, and when something exciting makes these emotions change direction, the first Word is canceled out. The emotions, which are fleshly, take precedence over the implanted Word.

As for what was sown among thorns, this is he who hears the Word, but the cares of the world and the pleasure and delight and glamour and deceitfulness of riches choke and suffocate the Word, and it yields no fruit.

—MATTHEW 13:22

But be doers of the Word [obey the message], and not merely listeners to it, betraying yourselves [into deception by reasoning contrary to the Truth]. For if anyone only listens to the Word without obeying it and being a doer of it, he is like a man who looks carefully at his [own] natural face in a mirror; for he thoughtfully observes himself, and then goes off and promptly forgets what he was like.

—JAMES 1:22–24

God's Mirror

If we don't walk away from God's mirror, forgetting what we just saw, we will see ourselves as God does. (See James 1:22–24.) We will glimpse the truth about ourselves. His Word will tell us what to do. God's mirror reflects the invisible things that are hidden in our hearts, such as our motives, our attitudes, our affections, our thoughts, our ambitions, our insecurities.

1.   What aspect of yourself have you seen reflected in God's mirror lately? (Is there something in particular that you have felt convicted of—or commended for?)

_____

_____

_____

2. What word from God do you need to act on?

_____

_____

People who do not have the "new heart" hear the truth and then start deceiving themselves about it. They rationalize what they have heard and come up with reasons why "this is not what the Bible means." Furthermore, they become deceived into thinking that they have all they need.

Clearly, we need "good soil" before we can expect God's truth to take root in us and grow.

GOOD SOIL

As for what was sown on good soil, this is he who hears the Word and grasps and comprehends it; he indeed bears fruit and yields in one case a hundred times as much as was sown, in another sixty times as much, and in another thirty.

—MATTHEW 13:23

The person with "good soil" has a converted heart. This person, who has received a new heart, has an active Word on the inside. God's spoken Word comes alive and produces good fruit.

The penetrating Word is filled with power! It energizes your spirit, heart, and soul as it accomplishes God's will. This Word goes down into the intricate parts of the inner man and "dissects" everything it finds there. When the enemy comes in "like a flood," that Word knows how to swim. When the fire rages, that Word knows how to hold its breath. When the wind starts blowing, that Word is anchored. When the sun starts to blaze, that Word knows how to get in the shade—regardless of what life's temperature may be.

New Heart Scale

Does your heart provide good soil for the implanted Word? Or is it hard and rocky and full of thorns? As you rate your heart on the scale, remember that *God can change your soil*—which is another way of saying He can give you a new heart. (You probably won't rate yourself with a "1" or a "10," which represent the uttermost extremes.) The "1" represents a totally depraved heart—which means you would not be reading this book!—and the "10" signifies that you have entered heaven already. Most of us will rate ourselves somewhere in the middle, between 3 and 8, which would mean you consider yourself to be somewhere between "seeking God about the new heart" and "impressed with the results and proceeding with new life."

Old Heart ◀ · ▶ *New Heart*

1 — 2 — 3 — 4 — 5 — 6 — 7 — 8 — 9 — 10

When the Word takes up residence in good soil, it operates with divine power and produces more fruit. The "good soil heart" embraces the Word it has received and produces more than it has been given.

"PREY"—OR PRAY?

Here is the problem: when the church does not step over into the spirit realm and receive this "new heart," then we sit idly by and become prey to the enemy. The church has been preaching the gospel, but we have not been preaching conversion. People are sitting in churches like "prey" in the pews. We have been telling them about where they need to be, but we do not have the power to get them there! We haven't told them the first step—how to get a new heart from God so the words we preach can take root in them.

What is the answer to the problem? We need to preach the whole message. We need to learn the *how to* along with the *what to*. We cannot live the gospel message without a new heart. We need a heart transplant.

Memory Verse

I have inclined my heart to perform Your statutes forever, even to the end.

—PSALM 119:112

Heart to Heart

Reach God's heart by writing another short prayer to Him. Choose one of the prayer-starters below, depending on your situation:

1.   *God, I want to confess to You that I am operating out of an unconverted heart. I have problems such as . . .*

_____

_____ .

I'm beginning to see that my old heart needs to be replaced. Help me, please, to cooperate with Your Spirit and to take the next steps. In Jesus' name, amen.

2.   *God, I believe I have received a new heart. However, I haven't taken very good care of it, and I can see some problems, such as . . .*

_____ .

I want to turn my heart over to You again. Please provide me with new faith and give me a fresh start. In Jesus' name, amen.

 H E A R T ᴮ E A T H E A R T ᴮ E A T H E A R T ᴮ E A T

Your heart—whether it's been made new or not—affects everything in your life.

CHAPTER 3

The Prophecy Begins

BECAUSE I HAVE been called to the office of prophet in the church, God began dealing with me long before I really grabbed hold of His Word to me about my need for a new heart. Sometimes in the middle of the night or during my prayer time, the Lord would speak to me, "Juanita, you need a new heart." But I did not understand. I felt that I had it all together. I knew that there were some things I had to deal with, but I felt that I had been "working with it."

We all have areas that have become our strongholds, although the age we live in has taught us to consider these areas to be "only weaknesses." We hear many teachings and words along the lines of "Be encouraged," "It's OK," "That's your weakness," and "God understands." By all means, the Lord does understand. Yet I believe that when you hear a word from Him, you should begin to change inside. You shouldn't be feeling comfortable with the so-called weaknesses of your old heart.

Blessed are the pure in heart: for they shall see God.
—MATTHEW 5:8, KJV

TRANSFORMING PRAYER

Several years ago, my life began to take a turn when God called me to pray at 5:00 a.m. each morning. As I sought the Lord with intensity, I began to change. One of the first scriptures He led me to was Matthew 5:8: "Blessed are the pure in heart: for they shall see God" (KJV). I had read this verse from the beatitudes many times. I had always interpreted it to mean, "Blessed are the pure in heart: for one day, when we die and go to heaven, we shall see God." The Lord began to say to me, "I desire that your spiritual eyes see Me *now*, but the only way that I can reveal My mysteries to you is according to My Word. I will not reveal My secrets to those whose hearts and motives are not pure." Then He added, "I am compelling you to get a new, pure heart."

I tried to respond by saying, "Well, I am struggling, and I see some things. I know that everything in my heart is not right. God, I just want You to fix it." But God showed me that He had no desire to reconstruct and "fix" my old heart. His desire and purpose was to give me a new heart. He took me to Luke 6:45:

> The upright (honorable, intrinsically good) man out of the good treasure [stored] in his heart produces what is upright (honorable and intrinsically good), and the evil man out of the evil storehouse brings forth that which is depraved (wicked and intrinsically evil); for out of the abundance (overflow) of the heart his mouth speaks.

When I listened to the language that came out of my mouth and observed some of my actions, I began to realize that a "fixed" heart would be of no use. I needed a new, upright heart. If you want to know what your heart is full of, listen to your conversation.

Heart Speech

For out of the abundance of the heart, the mouth speaketh.
—MATTHEW 12:34; LUKE 6:45, KJV

To see whether your heart's abundance consists of good or evil, have you learned to "read between the lines" of your speech? Consider the following:

Anxiety, fear (Read Philippians 4:6; 2 Timothy 1:7; 1 John 4:18.)

1. Describe how your speech—including how you talk to yourself—might betray anxiety or fear:

_____

_____

2. Today, how can you come closer to following Paul's advice in Philippians 4:6, "Do not fret or have any anxiety about anything"?

_____

_____

Patience, security (Read Romans 14:1; 1 Corinthians 13:4; 1 Thessalonians 5:14.)

1. Give an example of a time you were patient recently. (Note: When you are being patient, your "speech" may consist of no words at all!)

_____

_____

2. When you feel secure, you are better able to "help the weak" and be patient with them. What is the root of true security?

_____

_____

Bitter anger (Read Isaiah 58:9–10; 1 Corinthians 13:5; Ephesians 4:31; Hebrews 12:15.)

1. Describe a situation, past or present, when you "kept a record of wrongs" that had been done to you.

_____

_____

_____

2. Recall a time when you have been able to forgive someone who wronged you.

_____

_____

3. How does bitter anger shut down God's Spirit in our hearts?

_____

_____

Kindness, mercy, grace (Read Romans 2:4; 1 Corinthians 13:4; Ephesians 2:1–7; 4:32.)

1. How does God's kindness lead us to repentance? (See Romans 2:4 and Ephesians 2:1–7.)

_____

_____

2. How are God's kindness, mercy, and grace mirrored in the kindness, mercy, and grace we show to other people?

_____

_____

CRY LOUD AND SPARE NOT

God began to reveal to me that the "old heart" does not come with forgiveness in it. The old heart does not come with mercy. The old heart does not come with compassion. The old heart is born to be unfaithful to God. It is born without submissiveness. The nature of the old heart is to operate from a spirit of rebellion—everything is conditional.

Some prophets are called to prophesy "good." Some prophets are called to prophesy prosperity. But I am called to stand on the wall. I am called to cry loud and spare not. I am called to make

God's people aware that while they are getting a new house, a new car, and a new job, they need to be trying to get a new heart. The new heart causes us to see the things of God.

This new heart message is not as popular as the "relaxed" gospel we are hearing preached in this day. The church is becoming very cosmetic. We have taken on the "cloak" of the world to such a degree that the world feels comfortable coming to the God we preach about. People are coming to Him because the God we preach, after all, does not require us to sell out.

Today's religion says, "Come as you are and stay as you are. It is just between you and God, because God understands." Watch out! The Bible says that in the last days, the hearts of men will "wax cold," and they will not "endure sound doctrine" (Matt. 24:12, KJV; 2 Tim. 4:3, KJV). Sound doctrine *converts* men's hearts.

I'm dead set against prophets who substitute illusions for visions and use sermons to tell lies.... The fact is that they've lied to my people. They've said, "No problem; everything's just fine," when things are not at all fine. When people build a wall, they're right behind them slapping on whitewash. Tell those who are slapping on the whitewash, "When a torrent of rain comes and the hailstones crash down and the hurricane sweeps in and the wall collapses, what's the good of the whitewash that you slapped on so liberally, making it look so good?"
—EZEKIEL 13:8–12, THE MESSAGE

GOD IS NOT HIDDEN

When we have a pure heart, God is not hidden. When we have a new, pure heart, we can still see God even when everything looks

Getting Personal

About ten years ago, I really hit bottom. I was forced to get some help. I was really messed up. Unfortunately, one of my "helpers" said something to me that nobody should be allowed to say: "You know what? You are so broken that even God can't help you." It seemed to be true, though. I almost gave up.

But God sent two faithful friends who were patient and understanding in the face of my hopelessness. I tried to fend them off, but they could see past my depressed anger into my hurting heart, and they kept bringing me to God to see if enough of His love could soak into me that I could be healed.

My friends cared for me, but they didn't expect God to heal me so thoroughly. They knew He was a Healer, and they expected Him to fix my broken heart, mind, and body. But once I tasted the first drop of His kindness, I followed it to its source—and I discovered a whole new existence. He did heal me, but I don't think He just patched me up. He seems to have given me a heart transplant. My shattered old heart didn't even have any love left in it. Now, "Love" is my middle name. This new heart doesn't show any signs of deterioration, and it's been nine years now.

—C. L.

chaotic. But before we have a new heart, we are like the Pharisees. Jesus had strong words about the Pharisees:

> Woe to you, scribes and Pharisees, pretenders (hypocrites)! For you give a tenth of your mint and dill and cummin, and have neglected and omitted the weightier (more important) matters of the Law—right and justice and mercy and fidelity. These you ought [particularly] to have done, without neglecting the others. You blind guides, filtering out a gnat and gulping down a camel! Woe to you, scribes and Pharisees, pretenders (hypocrites)! For you clean the outside of the cup and of the plate, but within they are full of extortion (prey, spoil, plunder) and grasping self-indulgence. You blind Pharisee! First clean the inside of the cup and of the plate, so that the outside may be clean also. Woe to you, scribes and Pharisees, pretenders (hypocrites)! For you are like

See the Pharisee

We should not be shocked to discover that we have some traits in common with the Pharisees. Let's decide, with God's help, NOT to remain stuck in those traits. In your Bible, look up the scriptures in parentheses below. (The New International Version was used to create these questions.) As you fill in the blanks, ask yourself, "Do I see any Pharisee in myself?"

1. Do I keep asking the Lord to prove Himself to me, demanding to see _____ _____ (Matt. 12:38)?

2. Do I break God's _____ for the sake of my traditions, habits, or assumptions (Matt. 15:3)?

3. Do I get _____ when I hear that my words betray evil thoughts (Matt. 15:12, 18–19)?

4. Do I _____ what I preach (Matt. 23:3)?

5. Are my actions determined by what I want others to _____ (Matt. 23:5)?

6. Do I _____ _____ gnats but _____ a camel? In other words, do I keep up appearances but miss the main point (Matt. 23:24)?

7. Do I _____ the outside of myself, but inside remain full of _____ _____ and _____ (Matt. 23:25)?

8. Do I have a hard time believing my sins can be _____ (Matt. 9:2–6)?

tombs that have been whitewashed, which look beautiful on the outside but inside are full of dead men's bones and everything impure. Just so, you also outwardly seem to people to be just and upright but inside you are full of pretense and lawlessness and iniquity.

—MATTHEW 23:23–28

The Lord is saying to us that a person's pure, hidden heart is a lot more important to Him than a person's religiosity.

The Lord said to Samuel . . . The Lord sees not as a man sees; for man looks on the outward appearance, but the Lord looks on the heart.

—1 Samuel 16:7

EXPOSING THE DECEPTION OF THE OLD HEART

God told me, "I want you to begin to 'major' in what I am majoring in right now. It is a fact that I am taking My people along a certain route, and I am blessing them. I am allowing them to get the things that their hearts desire, because this will be the catalyst that I will use to prove to them that it was never Me they wanted. They wanted Me for things—they wanted Me for a car, they wanted Me for a house, they wanted Me for a job and for a new husband. When I give them everything that their heart desires, and when a newfound walk in Me does not come out of that, or a new heart, then I am showing them that they were never after a walk of righteousness when they came to Me."

Instead of a walk of righteousness, it is a wandering walk. As Jeremiah recorded, "This is what the Lord says about this people: 'They greatly love to wander; they do not restrain their feet. So the Lord does not accept them" (Jer. 14:10, NIV).

Even though we are doing many wonderful things in the body of Christ, God is sending us a warning. We must be careful that while we are prophesying prosperity and peace, God is not moving in a whole different vein!

God is compelling me to cry out to His people to provoke them to desire a true and pure heart, a new heart, a new start. It doesn't matter how many other prophets cry out "Blessings!" or "Peace," I must cry out this message.

_____

Then the Lord said to me, The [false] prophets prophesy lies in My name. I sent them not, neither have I commanded them, nor have I spoken to them. They prophesy to you a false or pretended vision, a worthless divination [conjuring or practicing magic, trying to call forth the responses supposed to be given by idols], and the deceit of their own minds. Therefore thus says the Lord concerning the [false] prophets who prophesy in My name— although I did not send them—and who say, Sword and famine shall not be in this land: By sword and famine shall these prophets be consumed.

—JEREMIAH 14:14–15

_____

Wandering Feet

1.   Read Jeremiah 14:10. From your personal experience, cite an example of "wandering feet" (yours or someone else's):

_____

_____

_____

2.   Did the owner of the wandering feet eventually "restrain" them and return to God's path?

_____

_____

Be especially careful when you are trying to be good so that you don't make a performance out of it. It might be good theater, but the God who made you won't be applauding.

When you do something for someone else, don't call attention to yourself. You've seen them in action, I'm sure—"playactors" I call them—treating prayer meeting and street corner alike as a stage, acting compassionate as long as someone is watching, playing to the crowds. They get applause, true, but that's all they get. When you help someone out, don't think about how it looks. Just do it—quietly and unobtrusively. That is the way your God, who conceived you in love, working behind the scenes, helps you out.

And when you come before God, don't turn that into a theatrical production either. All these people making a regular show out of their prayers, hoping for stardom! Do you think God sits in a box seat?

—MATTHEW 6:1–5, THE MESSAGE

WE CANNOT HIDE FROM THE TRUTH

We will still try to cover it up, over and over again saying, "I am not like that." Eventually, though, we will have to face the fact that we have become like the Pharisees.

You cannot hide who you really are. Eventually, that old heart within you will go into full operation. You cannot suppress it. You cannot keep that evil heart from operating. Its nature is to pump.

Everything is naked before Him to whom we must give an account. (See Hebrews 4:13.) God is calling us today to *get real and pursue the new heart.*

You cannot keep that evil heart from operating. Its nature is to pump.

Memory Verse

A new heart will I give you and a new spirit will I put within you, and I will take away the stony heart out of your flesh and give you a heart of flesh.

—EZEKIEL 36:26

Heart to Heart

O Lord, when I notice my speech patterns, I can detect my heart patterns. I can see _____ _____, _____, *and* _____ .

I want to desire You more. Please show me the next step of surrender. In Jesus' strong name, amen.

H E A R T ^B E A T H E A R T ^B E A T H E A R T ^B E A T

God wants you to become desperate for a new heart, not to settle for a reconstructed, "fixed" heart.

CHAPTER 4

The Prophetic Word Deepens

GOD TOOK ME to Ezekiel 13 to help me understand that, as a prophet in this hour, I could no longer keep my mouth shut. I could no longer silence the heartbeat of God.

> Hear the word of the Lord! Thus says the Lord God: Woe to the foolish prophets who follow their own spirit [and things they have not seen] and have seen nothing!…They have seen falsehood and lying divination, saying, The Lord says; but the Lord has not sent them. Yet they have hoped and made men to hope for the confirmation of their word.
> —EZEKIEL 13:2–3, 6

PROPHETS WHO PROPHESY FALSE HOPE

Prophets who prophesy false hope to the people give them the impression that God is "understanding" of their spiritual lethargy and that He wants to give them peace about the lives they are leading. Nothing could be further from the truth!

Such prophets have not spoken what God is saying. Such a message lands people in a final state of hopelessness.

Have you not seen a false vision and have you not spoken a lying divination when you say, The Lord says, although I have not spoken? Therefore thus says the Lord God: Because you have spoken empty, false, and delusive visions and have seen

> *lies, therefore, behold, I am against you, says the Lord God. And*
> *My hand shall be against the prophets who see empty, false, and*
> *delusive visions and who give lying prophecies....Because, even*
> *because they have seduced My people, saying, Peace, when there*
> *is no peace, and because when one builds a [flimsy] wall, behold,*
> *[these prophets] daub it over with whitewash, say to them who*
> *daub it with whitewash that it shall fall!*
> —EZEKIEL 13:7–11

God's prophets, His watchmen, do not speak the truth to these people about their need to go deeper in God. When we stand back and watch people build flimsy walls, seduced by the glamour of the world, then turn around and say, "That is good. At least you are not where you used to be. That is wonderful. You are doing fine," it is like daubing a flimsy cardboard wall with whitewash. What will happen to that wall when the rains come? (See Ezekiel 13:11.)

When the storms of life are blowing and the enemy comes in, many fall by the wayside. They have only the outward appearance of strength. They have no depth in God because they have not yet received the new heart.

YOU CANNOT LEAD PEOPLE FURTHER
THAN YOU HAVE GONE

When God has set you into a position, you can only preach from the realm in which you walk. You can only raise another person up to your own level. The depth of your own deliverance is the depth of deliverance you can offer to another.

If you are in a position to raise others up, it is a very serious matter. You had better be walking in the new heart, or God will afflict you until you understand how to walk! The Word of the Lord comes: "When I look and see those whom I have chosen before the

The Prophetic Word Deepens   49

The Seduction of Wishful Thinking

Can you think of some false messages you have heard (or preached)? You might not be able to think of an example for every category below.

Example of a false message about prosperity:

_____

_____

Example of a false message about physical health:

_____

_____

Example of a false message about a moral decision:

_____

_____

Example of a false message about God's judgment of sin:

_____

_____

Example of a false message about success:

_____

_____

foundation of the world to be born again and transformed, and I see a false prophet trying to help them construct something that is not going to be able to stand, then I have no other choice but to send a wind to blow it down. That wind will keep blowing it down. It will keep you in the realm of affliction to show you that you do not need structure only—you need a deposit. You need to be transformed. You need to be converted. There is a greater depth, a greater height, to which I am calling you." Thus says the Lord!

> *So will I break down the wall that you have daubed with whitewash and bring it down to the ground, so that its foundations will be exposed; when it falls, you will perish and be consumed in the midst of it. And you will know (understand and realize) that I am the Lord. Thus will I accomplish My wrath upon the wall and upon those who have daubed it with whitewash, and I will say to you, The wall is no more, neither are they who daubed it, the [false] prophets of Israel who prophesied deceitfully about Jerusalem, seeing visions of peace for her when there is no peace, says the Lord God.*
>
> —EZEKIEL 13:14–16

GOD LED ME INTO A DEATH WALK

When God began to say to me, "I want you to preach the new heart," then there had to be a death realm for me. There had to be an "exposing" for me. I had to come to the realization, publicly, that I needed a new heart and that there were things going on inside of me that did not please God.

If you come to the place where you say, "I am called of God

Getting Personal

"Once upon a time..." There was a time when I believed the fairy tale that said the goal of the Christian life is to live in a storybook palace. I believed that when I had acquired enough beautiful things, success, affluence, and even a handsome prince, it would prove I had followed God all right. Even if it didn't prove I had followed God, I felt that the more of those things I achieved and acquired, the more secure I'd be. My worries would be over.

I needed to outgrow that fairy tale and get real! In fact, I needed to realize that, regardless of the prominent voices that might be promoting the fairy tale, having those goals—while claiming to belong to Jesus—was almost worse than being a nonbeliever. Glitter is alluring, but glitter tarnishes.

—K. B.

to prophesy," "I am called of God to be a teacher," or "I am called of God to preach the gospel to the poor and to open blind eyes and set the captives free," then at some point, you will be compelled to give up your own idea of your life, even your reputation if necessary. You cannot hold on to your own life and walk around as if you have done nothing wrong, as if everything in your life is perfect.

We have the gospel backwards. We say to those who are compromising and living close to the edge of the world, "You are wonderful; you are going to be all right." But to people who are dying to the flesh and giving up all to follow God, we say, "You are going too deep." "You pray too much." "You are a little too righteous." "You are going a little too far off the deep end." "Be careful; you'll drive yourself crazy by praying every day for two or three hours."

We are pronouncing death to people who are selling out to God, and we are pronouncing life to people who walk in carnality according to the spirit of this world. When we do this, we are blinded by the old heart.

If you do not lead people to the kind of surrender that results in a new heart, God will be forced to deliver them from you.

Because with lies you have made the righteous sad and disheartened, whom I have not made sad or disheartened, and because you have encouraged and strengthened the hands of the wicked, that he should not return from his wicked way and be saved [in that you falsely promised him life], therefore you will no more see false visions or practice divinations, and I will deliver My people out of your hand. Then you will know (understand and realize) that I am the Lord.

—EZEKIEL 13:22–23

Heartache

If we understand God's ways, we will realize that walking with Him means we will suffer sometimes. Our new heart will not always feel happy. New hearts know what pain and trouble feel like. "To this you were called, because Christ suffered for you, leaving you an example, that you should follow in his steps" (1 Pet. 2:21, NIV).

Look deeper into the sorrowful aspect of the new heart:

1. "I do wish, brother, that I [Paul] may have some benefit from you in the Lord; refresh my heart in Christ" (Philem. 20, NIV).

Why do you think Paul's heart needed refreshing?

_____

_____

Did Philemon ease his heart? (See verse 21.)

_____

2. "Now my [Jesus'] heart is troubled, and what shall I say? 'Father, save me from this hour'? No, it was for this very reason I came to this hour" (John 12:27, NIV).

Why was Jesus' heart troubled?

_____

_____

What did His troubled heart cause Him to do?

_____

_____

3. "I [Paul] have great sorrow and unceasing anguish in my heart. For I could wish that I myself were cursed and cut off from Christ for the sake of my brothers, those of my own race" (Rom. 9:2–3, NIV).

Why was Paul's heart sorrowful?

_____

_____

What did his sorrow motivate him to do?

_____

_____

4. "They [Ephesian elders] all wept as they embraced him [Paul] and kissed him. What grieved them most was his statement that they would never see his face again" (Acts 20:37–38, NIV).

How are love and grief connected?

_____

_____

How are love and courage connected?

_____

_____

5. "When we [Luke, Philip, and other believers at Caesarea] heard this, we and the people there pleaded with Paul not to go up to Jerusalem. Then Paul answered, 'Why are you weeping and breaking my heart? I am ready not only to be bound, but also to die in Jerusalem for the name of the Lord Jesus'" (Acts 21:12–13, NIV).

Was Paul's heart breaking because he was headed for prison and death?

_____

_____

Why were the people upset?

_____

_____

THE TIME FOR CHANGE HAS COME

As pastors, teachers, or prophets in this hour of preaching the gospel, we should be feeling the temperature of the spirit realm. Crying out to the hearts of God's people, we must say, according to Hebrews 3:12–13:

[Therefore beware] brethren, take care, lest there be in any one of you a wicked, unbelieving heart [which refuses to cleave to, trust in, and rely on Him], leading you to turn away and desert or stand aloof from the living God. But instead warn (admonish, urge, and encourage) one another every day, as long as it is called Today, that none of you may be hardened [into settled rebellion] by the deceitfulness of sin [by the fraudulence, the stratagem, the trickery which the delusive glamour of his sin may play on him].

We need to be careful lest we have the "form of godliness," but we are "denying the power thereof" (2 Tim. 3:5, KJV). The real power is being able to say *yes* to God and *no* to the devil.

Have you ever wondered why Jesus had His disciples walk with Him at all times? It was necessary for the disciples to learn how to follow His steps. They needed to observe Him walking in the paths of the Father in order to learn to operate in signs, wonders, and miracles. The disciples learned how to submit by watching Jesus' example. He showed them how to be persecuted without warring back. (See Matthew 5:39.) He showed them how to suffer for righteousness' sake. (See Matthew 5:10.)

Jesus lived a pattern. As a result, Peter and Paul and the others knew how to suffer persecution, and they knew how to die. The disciples and early followers of Jesus understood the pattern and knew how to stand in the battle of the Lord.

PREACH THE NEW HEART MESSAGE

"Now you have closely observed and diligently followed my teaching, conduct, purpose in life, faith, patience, love, steadfastness..." (2 Tim. 3:10). Paul is describing a person who has received the new heart. This is the only kind of person who can

Persecution

Remember that I told you, A servant is not greater than his master [is not superior to him]. If they persecuted Me, they will also persecute you.

—JOHN 15:20

Blessed and happy and enviably fortunate and spiritually prosperous (in the state in which the born-again child of God enjoys and finds satisfaction in God's favor and salvation, regardless of his outward conditions) are those who are persecuted for righteousness' sake (for being and doing right), for theirs is the kingdom of heaven! Blessed (happy, to be envied, and spiritually prosperous—with life-joy and satisfaction in God's favor and salvation, regardless of your outward conditions) are you when people revile you and persecute you and say all kinds of evil things against you falsely on My account.

—MATTHEW 5:10–11

1. What is (or was) your first reaction to the idea that persecution will be part of your Christian walk?

_____

_____

2. Is there a difference between being "persecuted because of righteousness' sake" and being persecuted for a cause? In God's eyes, can they be the same?

_____

_____

3. According to the verses in Matthew, what is the reward for persecution?

_____

4. Is it a natural human trait to be happy when you are persecuted?

_____

_____

5. How do these verses accentuate the fact that we must have a new heart to live this way?

6. Here are some forms persecution can take. Can you think of some other scriptural examples of these types of persecution?

- Insults, slander—Isaiah 51:7; Matthew 5:11; 1 Peter 3:16; 1 Corinthians 4:12

- Physical abuse—Mark 14:65; Acts 16:22; 21:31–32

- Rejection—Psalm 119:141; Luke 6:22; John 9:22

- Murder—Matthew 24:9, Acts 7:57–8:1; 22:4

- Imprisonment—Acts 4:2; 5:2; 16:23; 22:4

7. What other forms of persecution can Christians suffer?

preach this message. You cannot preach about diligence, good conduct, purpose in life, faith, patience, love, and steadfastness unless you have first received these characteristics from God.

Then Paul goes deeper. He says his listeners have also

observed his "persecutions, sufferings—such as occurred to me at Antioch, at Iconium, and at Lystra, persecutions I endured, but out of them all the Lord delivered me" (v. 11).

That's right. People who preach the new heart will be persecuted. Paul elaborates: "In fact, everyone who wants to live a godly life in Christ Jesus will be persecuted, while evil men and impostors will go from bad to worse, deceiving and being deceived. But as for you, continue in what you have learned and have become convinced of" (vv. 12–14, NIV).

> *Now you have closely observed and diligently followed my teaching, conduct, purpose in life, faith, patience, love, steadfastness, persecutions, sufferings—such as occurred to me at Antioch, at Iconium, and at Lystra, persecutions I endured, but out of them all the Lord delivered me. Indeed all who delight in piety and are determined to live a devoted and godly life in Christ Jesus will meet with persecution [will be made to suffer because of their religious stand].*
>
> —2 TIMOTHY 3:10–12

As people believe the new heart message, they will suffer. As we deliver the new heart message, we will suffer. But messengers who have new hearts walk with Jesus. He shows us the pattern for how to walk with the new heart, and He delivers us from harm.

Paul reminds us, "Every Scripture is God-breathed (given by His inspiration) and profitable for instruction, for reproof and conviction of sin, for correction of error and discipline in obedience, [and] for training in righteousness (in holy living, in conformity to God's will in thought, purpose, and action)" (2 Tim. 3:16). God inspired all the scriptures about persecution and suffering. They are not in there by accident. We can expect hardship. Suffering will accomplish two things: it will convince us that we need new hearts, and it will purify our hearts and keep them pure.

God is charging you with this truth:

> I charge [you] in the presence of God and of Christ Jesus, Who is to judge the living and the dead, and by (in the light of) His coming and His kingdom: Herald and preach the Word! Keep your sense of urgency [stand by, be at hand and ready], whether the opportunity seems to be favorable or unfavorable. [Whether it is convenient or inconvenient, whether it is welcome or unwelcome, you as preacher of the Word are to show people in what way their lives are wrong.] And convince them, rebuking and correcting, warning and urging and encouraging them, being unflagging and inexhaustible in patience and teaching. For the time is coming when [people] will not tolerate (endure) sound and wholesome instruction, but, having ears itching [for something pleasing and gratifying], they will gather to themselves one teacher after another to a considerable number, chosen to satisfy their own liking and to foster the errors they hold.
>
> —2 TIMOTHY 4:1–3

Memory Verse

Declare to the people the whole doctrine concerning this Life (the eternal life which Christ revealed).

—ACTS 5:20

Heart to Heart

Expand this prayer to express to God what is in your heart:

God, I ask You to bind the enemy of my soul from coming upon me with fear to keep me from making a righteous stand. Protect me from _____

_____

_____.

Deliver me when I suffer persecution. Hear my heart's cry for help:

_____

_____

Make me a useful vessel for Your Spirit. Clean me inside and out.

_____

_____

_____

Amen and amen.

H E A R T B E A T H E A R T B E A T H E A R T B E A T

**Tell others God's truth, even when it might make you unpopular.
Don't stand by and allow people to miss what God is saying.**

CHAPTER 5

The Heart: Who Can Know It?

WHEN THE LORD first began telling me about my need for a new heart, I did not want to hear it. I had already seen the signs of my own shortcomings, but I felt they were just part of the makeup of my character. In reality, I was taking the easy way out.

THE GRACE FACTOR

Like many believers, I was abusing the "grace factor" in my walk with God. I assumed a comfortable position where I did not have to change certain behaviors because I knew that God's grace is available. Through my own spiritual laziness, I was using the liberty of Christ as an occasion for the flesh. This approach to life is addressed in Romans 6:1–2: "Are we to remain in sin in order that God's grace (favor and mercy) may multiply and overflow? Certainly not! How can we who died to sin live in it any longer?"

Even as I began to recognize "personality traits" for what they were—sinful evidence of an old heart—I would simply say, "Lord, forgive me." But the traits would resurface—sometimes on a daily basis. God was giving me opportunities to allow my mind to be transformed. But, like most people, instead of spending quality time to find out why these shortcomings kept surfacing, I took the comfortable way out. I attached those things to myself and made the excuse that they were "just part of my personality." "This is just the way I am." "God understands the way I am."

When you do this, your friends and associates begin to accept that behavior as just being "you." They adjust to it, making room for that part of you that has not been purified. As a result, you stay the way you are. Once people become accustomed to your "old heart" behavior, they avoid it. They make sure they do not do anything to bring that part of your temperament to the surface. If it surfaces, they say, "Well, that is just the way she is."

> *And don't say anything you don't mean.... You only make things worse when you lay down a smoke screen of pious talk, saying, "I'll pray for you," and never doing it, or saying "God be with you," and not meaning it. You don't make your words true by embellishing them with religious lace. In making your speech sound more religious, it becomes less true. Just say "yes" and "no." When you manipulate words to get your own way, you go wrong.*
>
> —MATTHEW 5:34–37, THE MESSAGE

The Lord began to make me understand that I was missing the point. My own heart was deceiving me. ("The heart is deceitful above all things," as Jeremiah 17:9 says.) Even after being raised in the church and being saved, I constantly "fell away," doing things that were outside of God's will. One indication of the self-deception was the way I was comparing myself to other people. I could always find someone who was "less all right" than I was. Or I would compare myself with someone and think, *Well, he and I, or she and I, are a lot alike, so I am not all that bad.*

> *The heart is deceitful above all things, and it is exceedingly perverse and corrupt and severely, mortally sick! Who can know it [perceive, understand, be acquainted with his own heart and mind]? I the Lord search the mind, I try the heart,*

Instruments of Righteousness

Read Romans 6:13–14.

1. Practically speaking, what does this scriptural command mean in your life?

_____

_____

_____

2. What parts of your body can you offer Him as instruments of righteousness?

_____

_____

3. What is your motivation for doing this? (See verse 14.)

_____

even to give to every man according to his ways, according to the fruit of his doings.

—Jeremiah 17:9–10

HOW DO YOU KNOW YOU NEED A NEW HEART?

If our hearts are so easily deceived, how will we ever know when we need a new heart?

Ephesians 4 shows you how. You need a new heart if…

1. You have a problem with "futile thinking," which is ineffective, useless, and unsuccessful. Your thought patterns do not yield anything that is fruitful or beneficial. You look at things your own way and pervert the Word of God.

Heart Examination

Taking the five characteristics of an old heart described in Ephesians 4:17–20, reflect on these questions:

1. How have I seen "futile thinking" in my life—useless thought patterns that are self-centered but do not yield benefit to myself or to others?

2. How has my moral understanding been darkened? Have I justified behavior that I knew was sinful?

3. Have I excused my behavior by using excuses drawn from psychology, my family history, or the prevailing behavior in the society around me?

What has been my favorite excuse?

4. What may I have done persistently and repeatedly that was my own "way of doing things"—to the possible detriment of myself and others?

5. How have I "talked the talk" on Sunday, only to not "walk the walk" Monday through Saturday?

2. Your moral understanding is darkened. When you do ungodly things and yet try to justify doing them, your moral understanding has been darkened and your reasoning is beclouded.

3. You explain away your actions according to worldly knowledge and carnal information. Along with the rest of this world, you are in a sweat to gain more information and knowledge, and then you use that information to explain your actions away.

4. You persistently do things your own way. You have become willfully blinded. You have chosen it. You have been doing something a certain way for years and years, until you finally believe that you are walking in God's ways, when in fact you are in error. Your heart has become hardened and insensitive to what is right.

5. You indulge in every impurity that comes your way. You may have learned the vocabulary of Scripture, but you have not learned Christ.

So I tell you this, and insist on it in the Lord, that you must no longer live as the Gentiles do, in the futility of their thinking. They are darkened in their understanding and separated from the life of God because of the ignorance that is in them due to the hardening of their hearts. Having lost all sensitivity, they have given themselves over to sensuality so as to indulge in every kind of impurity, with a continual lust for more. You,

however, did not come to know Christ that way. ("But ye have
not so learned Christ," KJV.)

EPHESIANS 4:17–2, NIV

THE DECEPTION OF THE FLESH

The flesh is you, in the natural, inside and out. The "internal" flesh is part of your old heart and your unrenewed mind, which causes the "external" flesh to disobey God.

Galatians 5:19–21 spells out the works of the flesh. Read closely:

> Now the doings (practices) of the flesh are clear (obvious): they are immorality, impurity, indecency, idolatry, sorcery, enmity, strife, jealousy, anger (ill temper), selfishness, divisions (dissensions), party spirit (factions, sects with peculiar opinions, heresies), envy, drunkenness, carousing, and the like. I warn you beforehand, just as I did previously, that those who do such things shall not inherit the kingdom of God.

These are just some of the characteristics of the old heart. The Spirit of the Lord does not govern the old heart because it does not belong to Him. It is the heart of Satan. So anything that Satan puts forth for us to do, if we have the old heart, we cannot rebuke it. We cannot say, "I refuse to do that," because we are housing his heart. We feel we are in control, but really Satan, through our corrupt hearts, is the one in charge.

However, praise God, He has not left us this way. He offers us a new heart with which we can live a new life. He puts His Word into our minds to tell us that we need transformation from God.

Getting Personal

It is easy for me to rationalize my way out of following God. When I read "extreme" scriptures such as Jeremiah 4:22 or Galatians 5:19–21, I excuse myself. I just don't think I am that bad.

But what if I am? What if it is like murder? I would be a murderer whether I had killed one person or one hundred. I could be a sinner even if I am dressed in white religious clothes.

If I have any suspicion that I might need a new heart, I probably do. Or I may need to pay serious attention to the new heart that I received from God but didn't take care of.

Bottom line: I have decided that I cannot go wrong by surrendering myself to God. Why should I try to protect myself from a God who loves me so much He sent His Son to die for me?

—A. H.

[O Lord] how long must I see the flag [marking the route for flight] and hear the sound of the trumpet [urging the people to flee for refuge]? [Their chastisement will continue until it has accomplished its purpose] for My people are stupid, says the Lord [replying to Jeremiah]; they do not know and understand Me. They are thickheaded children, and they have no understanding. They are wise to do evil, but to do good they have no knowledge [and know not how].

—Jeremiah 4:21–22

THE SPIRITUAL EMERGENCY ROOM

If you do not get a new heart, your old heart will ambush you. Before you realize it, you end up in the spiritual emergency room, manifesting signs of heart failure.

When everything starts folding in and coming against you, it's not God's fault. Your own rebellion toward God causes your atmosphere to turn. These changes are your vital signs, letting you know that it is time to receive a new heart.

Your ways and your doings have brought these things upon you. This is your calamity and doom; surely it is bitter, for surely it reaches your very heart. [It is not only the prophet but also the people who cry out in their thoughts] My anguish, my anguish! I writhe in pain! Oh, the walls of my heart! My heart is disquieted and throbs aloud within me; I cannot be silent! For I have heard the sound of the trumpet, the alarm of war.

—JEREMIAH 4:18–19

This is the sound of spiritual vital signs crying out, proving the truth of the familiar verse in Romans 6:23: "For the wages which sin pays is death."

I am speaking in familiar human terms because of your natural limitations. For as you yielded your bodily members [and faculties] as servants to impurity and ever increasing lawlessness, so now yield your bodily members [and faculties] once for all as servants to righteousness (right being and doing) [which leads] to sanctification. For when you were slaves of sin, you were free in regard to righteousness. But then what benefit (return) did you get from things of which you are now ashamed? [None] for the end of those things is death. But now since you have been set free from sin and have become the slaves of God, you have your present reward in holiness and its end is eternal life. For the wages which sin pays is death, but the [bountiful] free gift of God is eternal life through (in union with) Jesus Christ our Lord.

—ROMANS 6:19–23

DIVINE WARNINGS

God does not want us to be destroyed. He does not desire for us to be tormented by the ways of this world. Instead, He gives His people divine warnings to get their attention and to compel them to change their ways.

God never releases judgment without first sending a warning. This is why He is warning us, right now. He is telling us, "It is time to receive a new heart."

True Confessions

True confession leads to repentance, and repentance changes the heart. Read the following passages in your Bible: Luke 5:31–32; Acts 8:21–22; 3:19; 17:30; 2 Corinthians 7:10; Romans 2:4.

1.   How are confession and repentance different from each other?

_____

_____

2.   Can you have one without the other? _____

3.   How are confession and repentance related to each other?

_____

_____

_____

4.   Describe a time when you or someone close to you confessed a sin but did not change for the better:

_____

_____

_____

5. Describe a time when you or someone close to you confessed a sin and did change for the better:

_____

_____

_____

6. What was the underlying difference between the two situations? (What happened inside the heart?)

_____

_____

_____

> For I earnestly protested to and warned your fathers at the time that I brought them up out of the land of Egypt, even to this day, protesting to and warning them persistently, saying, Obey My voice. Yet they did not obey or incline their ear [to Me], but everyone walked in the stubbornness of his own evil heart. Therefore I brought upon them all [the calamities threatened in] the words of this covenant or solemn pledge, which I had commanded, but they did not do.
>
> —JEREMIAH 11:7–8

Obedience requires a combination of a new heart and a transformed mind. The heart understands, and the mind knows. When both are in operation, the good in the heart flows to the mind and trains it with "know-how" to live according to God's Word.

Divine warnings are the advance symptoms of heart failure. Therefore, when you receive a divine warning, you know when it is time for a change of heart. You know when that old heart is starting to break down.

In medical heart transplants, it is impossible to receive a new heart unless the old heart is failing you. You cannot get a new heart until the old one breaks down—until it is starting to destroy your life. Then, and only then, will doctors recommend you for a heart transplant.

Examine your heart right now. Ask yourself, "Is my heart destroying my life?" If so, you are a candidate for a heart transplant. But first, you have to get up and go to the Doctor in order to receive treatment. The Doctor has no way of knowing that you need a heart transplant unless you initiate treatment. You have to "confess" your need before the Doctor can help you. The breakdown of vital signs will lead you to this place.

God wants you to realize that you need a new heart. He is waiting for you to say, "I cannot survive with this old heart. It has destroyed everything around me. It is destroying everything within me. I cannot find comfort in You, God."

Is that the cry of your heart?

Memory Verse

For the wages which sin pays is death, but the [bountiful] free gift of God is eternal life through (in union with) Jesus Christ our Lord.

—ROMANS 6:23

Heart to Heart

W̲e can be sure that we are praying in a way that will reach God's heart when we use words that come straight from Scripture. For instance, a prayer drawn from Psalm 119:36–37 (NIV) can become an appropriate prayer for the end of this chapter:

Dear God, turn my heart toward Your statutes, and not toward selfish gain. Turn my eyes away from worthless things; preserve my life according to Your Word. Amen.

Find another psalm-prayer and make it your own prayer by writing it below:

_____

_____

_____

_____

_____

H E A R T B E A T H E A R T B E A T H E A R T B E A T

**God shows us that we need a new heart.
It's our responsibility to heed His warning.**

CHAPTER 6

A Scientific Point of View

WE ARE TRULY "fearfully and wonderfully made" (Ps. 139:14, KJV). Everything that God does in the spirit realm has an explanation, symbol, or example in the natural realm, because He is the Creator of both realms.

> But it is not the spiritual life which came first, but the physical and then the spiritual. The first man [was] from out of earth, made of dust (earthly-minded); the second Man [is] the Lord from out of heaven. Now those who are made of the dust are like him who was first made of the dust (earthly-minded); and as is [the Man] from heaven, so also [are those] who are of heaven (heavenly-minded). And just as we have borne the image [of the man] of dust, so shall we and so let us also bear the image [of the Man] of heaven.
>
> —1 CORINTHIANS 15:46–49

Let's examine how God has created our physical hearts so that we can better understand how we are created in the image of God's Spirit.

THE NATURAL HEART

Here are some amazing facts about our physical hearts. I have taken them from a book called *The HeartMath Solution,* by Doc Lew Childre and Howard Martin (published in 2000 by Harper SanFrancisco).

- The heart generally functions for seventy to eighty years without maintenance or replacement.
- During a lifetime, it beats about 100,000 times a day, which is about 40 million times a year or about 3 billion beats altogether.
- The heart pumps about 2 gallons of blood per minute, which is more than 100 gallons per hour.
- One person's vascular system is long enough to wrap around the earth two times—over 60,000 miles.
- The heart is like a power plant. It generates 5,000 times more energy than the brain.
- The heart has its own "brain." This "heart brain" has more than 40,000 nerve cells, the same number contained in many of the nerve centers below the cerebral cortex of the brain.
- The heart can keep beating without being connected to the brain. (For example, when someone has a heart transplant, the surgeons have to sever the nerves that run from the brain to the heart. When they put the heart into the new body, the surgeons restore the heartbeat without reconnecting the nerves, and it keeps beating.)

The natural heart sends emotional and intuitive signals to the brain and body that help to govern our lives. It produces a strong substance called *atrial natriuretic factor* (ANF) that helps to balance our bodies' systems. In a similar way, our new hearts balance us and help us see everything from a heavenly perspective. This strengthens our consciences and helps us to make wise and godly decisions.

For You did form my inward parts; You did knit me together in my mother's womb. I will confess and praise You for You are fearful and wonderful and for the awful wonder of my birth! Wonderful are Your works, and that my inner self knows right well.

—PSALM 139:13–14

Wonderfully Made

Re-read Psalm 139:13–14. Compare it with the following passages of Scripture:

"Your hands made me and formed me; give me understanding to learn your commands" (Ps. 119:73, NIV).

"This is what the Lord says—he who made you, who formed you in the womb, and who will help you" (Isa. 44:2, NIV).

"Who endowed the heart with wisdom or gave understanding to the mind?" (Job 38:36, NIV).

1. What is the answer to Job's question in Job 38:36?

_____

2. Are wisdom and understanding bestowed to every human heart as "standard equipment"?

_____

What must we do to obtain them? (See James 1:5.)

_____

3. The psalmist extols God: "Your works are wonderful" (Ps. 139:14). One of God's most wonderful works is His guarantee that He will help us. Copy a line from one of the scriptures above that supports this guarantee:

_____

_____

THE NATURAL MIND

The structures of the brain include the brain stem (medulla oblongata), an emotional center (amygdala), and logic centers (cerebral cortex and frontal lobes).

The medulla contains the nerve systems that regulate our heart rate, breathing, and other body functions. It monitors and facilitates communication to the heart, lungs, nervous system, and other parts of the body.

The amygdala stores emotional memories and compares these experiences with new information. It determines what is relevant to each individual and forms the brain's basis for our perceptions. This is why our imagination, strategies, and decisions are colored by our emotions. When emotions are balanced, they give life and meaning to facts, objectives, and logic. When they become unbalanced, they distort the truth.

The cerebral cortex reasons, reflects, evaluates, considers, strategizes, plans, and imagines. The frontal lobes handle decision making and determine which emotional response is appropriate for each situation.

The brain is always active, even while you are sleeping, sending neural messages through the medulla that can affect the rhythms of our hearts. The heart can also send messages back to the brain that can alter our consciousness and our actions.

The heart and mind operate together to remember everything. Even as expectant mothers talk and react, their words and actions are recorded into their unborn child's memory code. By the time that child is six months old, the record of his or her experiences has escalated at an unbelievable rate. This sets the pattern that runs throughout our lifetimes. Psychologists have proven that by the time a child reaches five years of age, his or her heart and mind patterns are basically set for life.

But as for you, O man of God, flee from all these things; aim at and pursue righteousness (right standing with God and true goodness), godliness (which is the loving fear of God and being Christlike), faith, love, steadfastness (patience), and gentleness of heart. Fight the good fight of the faith; lay hold of the eternal life to which you were summoned and [for which] you confessed the good confession [of faith] before many witnesses.

—1 Timothy 6:11–12

Getting Personal

By nature I am not one of those "hearts and flowers" kind of guys. I'm real down-to-earth, not romantic. But I started thinking about my *heart* after a big problem upset me. My wife kept using the word *heart* when she talked with me. She'd say, "You're just heartbroken." "Your heart's desire has been taken away." "I can feel your heartache." "You've got a heavy heart."

It kind of got to me. All kinds of junk were coming to the surface from deep inside me that I didn't know was there. I didn't want to have these "heart problems."

After a long, depressing time, I began to realize that my Christianity wasn't doing me much good, either. Where was this God who was supposed to be taking care of me?

Well, now I think He was just letting me have a bad enough time to get my attention. One night I just prayed, "Lord, please take this trashed heart of mine. I want a new heart. I can't figure out how to 'unbreak' this old one. When I get up out of my bed tomorrow, let me know that something is different."

You know what? It was different when I got up. God must like to hear prayers like that.

—J. J.

THE CONVERTED HEART

Now consider the spiritual heart. The converted heart longs to walk in the ways of God, which means that it "declares war" on the resident mind. The spiritual battle begins.

Do not be conformed to this world (this age), [fashioned after and adapted to its external, superficial customs],

Conscience

Your conscience is your sense of blamelessness (or guilt) regarding your behavior, thoughts, or general character. It takes a pure, new heart to create a pure, undefiled conscience. In the Old Testament, the word *conscience* is used only six times (in the New International Version). However, the word is found more than twenty-four times in the New Testament.

1. Can you think of an explanation for this disparity?

\
\

Read the following sampling of verses from the New Testament that use the word *conscience*: Acts 23:1; 24:16; Romans 9:1–2; 1 Corinthians 4:4; 10:25; 2 Corinthians 1:12; 4:2; 1 Timothy 1:5, 18–19; 3:9; 2 Timothy 1:3.

2. Which seven of these scriptures refer specifically to a good (pure, clear) conscience?

\
\

3. Which four of these scriptures refer to the conscience more as a sort of watchdog for the soul?

\
\

4. The same person is speaking in all of these passages. Who is it?

\

5. Think about this person's life story. Can you surmise why he would use this word so much?

\
\

but be transformed (changed) by the [entire] renewal of your mind [by its new ideals and its new attitude], so that you may prove [for yourselves] what is the good and acceptable and perfect will of God, even the thing which is good and acceptable and perfect [in His sight for you].

—ROMANS 12:2

The converted heart must precede a change of mind and a new perspective. The mind needs to be retrained with the understanding that is built into the new heart—which is the heart of God. The mind must be retrained through the Word of God. Then the emotional and rational memory banks will be refilled with godly information from the Bible.

SYNERGY OF HEART AND MIND

The new heart and the renewed mind are a powerful combination. We need to learn how to tap into their *synergy*, their combined action whose result is greater than the sum of the components.

When understanding flows from the new heart to the renewed mind, it causes the body to receive God's blessing. With heart and brain unified, you experience a natural flow, rhythm, and peace within.

We cannot let our minds control us. We must ask for a new heart and then begin to obey the divine messages that God sends from within us. When we do, we will walk in divine authority because we will be in sync with the way God intended us to be. And when we are in sync with what God intended, the devil has to flee from us when we resist him (James 4:7). The only thing that gives you control over the enemy is the synergy of the new heart and a renewed mind that is fully submitted to God and His will.

Surrender

Why is voluntary surrender our only option? If God is all-powerful, why doesn't He just crush our walls of pretense and human pride and take over?

One reason is that even if He invaded, our unsurrendered souls would mount guerilla warfare. In a misguided effort of self-preservation, our hard hearts and unrenewed minds would endeavor to sabotage His work of grace.

Read Romans 8:5-11 and Galatians 5:19-24.

1. What are some of the evidences of our sinful natures? (See Galatians 5:19-21.)

_____

_____

Would you say these qualities could help support "guerilla warfare"?

_____

2. What is the overall goal of our sinful natures?

_____

3. What is our goal if the Spirit of God dwells in us?

_____

4. What are some of the evidences of a new heart and renewed mind? (See Galatians 5:22-23.)

_____

_____

5. How do we get rid of our old sinful nature? (See Galatians 5:24.)

_____

_____

_____

Jesus gave us an example when He surrendered Himself for crucifixion.

So don't you see that we don't owe this old do-it-yourself life one red cent? There's nothing in it for us, nothing at all. The best thing to do is give it a decent burial and get on with your new life. God's Spirit beckons.

—ROMANS 8:12–14, THE MESSAGE

To the pure [in heart and conscience] all things are pure, but to the defiled and corrupt and unbelieving nothing is pure; their very minds and consciences are defiled and polluted. They profess to know God [to recognize, perceive, and be acquainted with Him], but deny and disown and renounce Him by what they do.

—TITUS 1:15–16

When your mind is submitted to the will of God, which flows from your new heart, then this heart begins to rule and dominate your flesh and influence your surroundings. Since God resides in your new heart, and the character of God is already in it, you are automatically placed in a seat above Satan. You do not have to pray to get there. Your new heart transforms you to your rightful place. As you surrender your mind on a daily basis, it keeps you there.

For those who are according to the flesh and are controlled by its unholy desires set their minds on and pursue those things which gratify the flesh, but those who are according to the Spirit and are controlled by the desires of the Spirit set their minds on and seek those things which gratify the [Holy] Spirit. Now the mind of the flesh [which is sense and reason without the Holy Spirit] is death [death that comprises all the miseries arising from sin, both here and hereafter]. But the mind of the [Holy] Spirit is life and [soul] peace [both now and forever]. [That *is] because the mind of the flesh [with its carnal thoughts and purposes] is hostile to God, for it does not submit itself to God's Law; indeed it cannot. So then those who are living the life of the flesh [catering to the appetites and impulses of their carnal nature] cannot please or satisfy God, or be acceptable to Him. But you are not living the life of the flesh, you are living the life of the Spirit, if the [Holy] Spirit of God [really] dwells with you [directs and controls you].... And if the Spirit of Him Who raised up Jesus from the dead dwells in you, [then] He Who raised up Christ from the dead will also restore to life your mortal (short-lived, perishable) bodies through His Spirit Who dwells in you.*

—ROMANS 8:5–9, 11

JESUS IS OUR EXAMPLE

Jesus came to the earth with the heart of God inside of Him. He still, however, could have aborted His assignment if He had made the wrong choices. He could have walked around, allowing His mind to dictate what He did or did not do and what He had the right to be. Since He was the Son of God, He could have demanded to be given a mansion, servants, wealth, and everything else—and it all would have happened—but He didn't. He chose, instead, to obey His Father's heart.

Jesus came into the earth with a dying heart. His goal was to die—to fulfill an eternal assignment. His heart was "new" from the beginning, and it was built with an assignment already in it. As He submitted to His Father's heart, He obeyed His Father's will.

When we are born again and receive the new heart, it comes with an assignment already in it. We need to do what Jesus did instead of letting our minds and bodies dictate what we have the "right" to do and be. We can "let go and let God."

Our heavenly Father is saying, "I want you to submit to obedience, because when you give up your right to be right in the natural realm, your new heart will be able to govern what you do from the spirit realm, and that is when you will have victory. That is when you will receive power to do what Jesus did."

Memory Verse

And He replied to him, You shall love the Lord your God with all your heart and with all your heart and with all your soul and with all your mind (intellect). This is the great (most important, principal) and first commandment. And a second is like it: You shall love your neighbor as [you do] yourself.

—MATTHEW 22:37–39

Heart to Heart

Father, I want to discard my old heart, which is killing me by degrees, and receive a transplanted, new heart from Your hand. I don't want to cling to my old heart's ways. Hear me as I surrender to You the evidences of my sinful nature:

_____

_____

_____

_____

_____

I want my heart to be set on You. Amen.

HEARTBEATHEARTBEATHEARTBEAT

Our new spiritual hearts and our renewed minds resemble our physical hearts and minds—they communicate with each other, and together they are powerful.

CHAPTER 7

Results of a Heart Transplant

WHEN YOU RECEIVE a new heart, you can expect a battle. Your flesh will not give up control without a fight.

The good news is that Jesus has overcome the world (John 16:33), and the healthy, new heart He has transplanted into us means we have Jesus, the One who died and rose again, in our innermost being.

But just as the person who receives a transplanted natural heart must engage in a fight to keep his or her body from rejecting that transplanted heart, so too the enemy tries to make us reject our new heart.

A DIVINE TRANSITION

God has provided us with the perfect heart Donor—Jesus. His heart is a heart of power. Jesus' heart came with an eternal assignment—and when we receive His heart, we receive our part of that mission.

If you have a new heart, you have the supernatural power that comes with it, but this is where the battle comes in. Whether you realize it or not, there has always been a battle for your soul.

Too many of us have functioned in this battle like prisoners of war. Stripped of our weapons and uniforms, we have been chained and thrown by the enemy into a pit of bondage where there is little or no food (the Word) and no rest. The enemy's cruel forced labor has drained every ounce of our strength. When the new heart sets us free, dresses us for battle, and puts us right back into active duty, some of us are like spiritual POWs who never overcome the trauma of war. Even after we have been rescued and brought back home, our minds torment us with reruns of what used to be. Though we have been set free, we are spiritually paralyzed. We do not even try to walk in our newfound freedom.

"Leprosy of the Heart"

For I am poor and needy, and my heart is wounded and stricken within me.
—PSALM 109:22

The hearts of prisoners of war (POWs) remain in captivity because they cannot break free on their own. Think of how Jesus healed lepers when He walked the earth. Those of us who are spiritual POWs have "leprosy of the heart." We need God to help us before we can receive a new heart. We feel isolated, even ostracized, and completely unable to change our circumstances.

Read these two accounts of Jesus healing lepers in the New Testament: Matthew 8:2–4; Luke 17:12–19.

• What did the lepers have to do to be healed?

_____

• Did Jesus rescind the healing of the nine lepers who didn't even remember to thank Him?

_____

• Do you think they kept their healings even if they neglected to go to the priest as Jesus told them to do? _____

Now read and review the story of the woman caught in adultery (John 8). As far as we know, she didn't particularly want her "captive heart" to be free until this humiliating public disclosure brought her face-to-face with a Savior who could give the courage and grace to change completely. He did not condemn her for being a captive. He offered her a way out.

• What did she have to do in order to stay free (v. 11)?

_____

_____

- Now think of your own situation. Do you feel you may have "leprosy of the heart"?

_____

- Based on the stories above, what can you expect from Jesus?

_____

- Very simply, what do you need to do?

_____

_____

Heal me, O Lord, and I shall be healed; save me and I shall be saved, for You are my praise.

—JEREMIAH 17:14

Your new heart, being the heart of God, has infinitely more power than anything else does. Change will come if you allow it. Are you ready to change?

If we trust and obey our new heart, Jesus will help us, step by step, to get rid of all our bondages. Philippians 1:6 says, "And I am convinced and sure of this very thing, that He Who began a good work in you will continue until the day of Jesus Christ [right up to the time of His return], developing [that good work] and perfecting and bringing it to full completion in you."

In other words, Jesus will work inside of you until you do consistently what is pleasing to God (Phil. 2:13). If you obey the Lord, your new heart will lead you through this life and into eternity. Things may feel strange at first, but if you will submit to God, He will do His "perfect work" in you (2 Tim. 3:16–17; James 1:4).

Therefore also now, says the Lord, turn and keep on coming to Me with all your heart, with fasting, with weeping, and with mourning [until every hindrance is removed and the broken fellowship is restored]. Rend your hearts and not your garments and return to the Lord, your God, for He is gracious and merciful, slow to anger, and abounding in loving-kindness; and He revokes His sentence of evil [when His conditions are met].

—Joel 2:12–13

Getting Personal

I never had much of a social life. I told myself and others that I was just shy and introverted. I graduated from high school and then just kept living with my mother, working at the same job I'd had during high school. I was unhappy all the time—and jealous, to tell the truth. It seemed like everyone had more of a life than I did. I felt stuck. I was tired of doing nothing. One day I fell into a conversation with an older Christian acquaintance at work. After she listened to my complaints for a while, she told me to read 2 Corinthians 12:10, but she wouldn't tell me what it said. So I went out on my lunch break to a bookstore to find a Bible. Here's how it reads in THE MESSAGE: "Now I take limitations in stride, and with good cheer, these limitations that cut me down to size—abuse, accidents, opposition, bad breaks. I just let Christ take over! And so the weaker I get, the stronger I become."

I turned over a new leaf that day. I let the Lord take over. He had a lot of retraining to do, but I am a much better person because of that decision. I am still somewhat shy, but I'm not so fearful or irritable. I have moved on, and I'm exploring some new opportunities. I don't ever want to return to that old way of life.

—F. T.

THE MIND DECLARES WAR

A paradigm shift is occurring. While your old mind is being renewed (as the result of obeying God's Word), your new heart is replacing the old actions and patterns in your brain. As you sow to the Spirit, you are taking ground that Satan once occupied.

Your mind perceives this as a threat, so you experience internal conflict. The apostle Paul said:

So I find it to be a law (rule of action of my being) that when I want to do what is right and good, evil is ever present with me and I am subject to its insistent demands. For I endorse and delight in the Law of God in my inmost self [with my new nature]. But I discern in my bodily members [in the sensitive appetites and wills of the flesh] a different law (rule of action) at war against the law of my mind (my reason) and making me a prisoner to the law of sin that dwells in my bodily organs [in the sensitive appetites and wills of the flesh].

—ROMANS 7:21–23

When you obey your new heart's rulership, the Word actually begins to renew your mind from within and from without. Your brain is sandwiched. You have the Word inside of you and are putting the Word into you (from outside) by reading the Bible. Old mind and heart patterns are literally being squeezed out. You feel the conflict inside of you.

It began even as you knelt at the altar deciding to follow Christ. Thoughts began to dart through your mind: *I cannot give this up. I am not ready to do this. I am afraid that So-and-so will not understand.* This was your first battle in the war of your new heart. Your mind keeps throwing out its alarm signals, the new heart responds by sending a wave of conviction, and the battle goes on.

Now the Lord is the Spirit, and where the Spirit of the Lord is, there is liberty (emancipation from bondage, freedom). And all of us, as with unveiled face, [because we] continued to behold [in the Word of God] as in a mirror the glory of the Lord, are constantly being transfigured into His very own image in ever increasing splendor and from one degree of glory to another; [for this comes] from the Lord [Who is] the Spirit.

—2 CORINTHIANS 3:17–18

Internal Conflict

Have you experienced the tug-of-war between your old mind and your new heart? These conflicts show that God is at work in you.

In his letter to the church in Rome, Paul wrote in detail about this conflict and about the freedom we have in Christ. His other letters, which were written to believers like you, also contain helpful insights into this conflict.

Read chapter 6 of Paul's letter to the Romans, in which Paul talks about how we become free of the domination of sin.

1.   What have we "died to" (vv. 2, 7)?

_____

2.   What happens after that death (vv. 4–5)?

_____

3.   Practically speaking, what does it mean to "consider yourselves also dead to sin and your relation to it broken, but alive to God" (v. 11)?

_____

_____

_____

4.   How is this like a medical heart transplant?

_____

_____

_____

5.   What is the "reward" for sin (v. 23)?

_____

6.   The same word can be used to describe the reward ("wages") for sin (v. 23) and the cure for sin (vv. 2, 7). What is the word?

_____

7. Who has made the cure for sin different from the results of the "wages" for sin?

_____

8. What is your part in this process (vv. 11–13)?

_____

_____

_____

9. Put Romans 6:5–6 into your own words, using "I" instead of "we," transforming these verses into a personal statement of faith:

_____

_____

10. Put Romans 6:11–14 into your own words, using "I" instead of "you," to transform these verses into a personal statement of intent.

_____

_____

_____

DO NOT QUENCH THE SPIRIT

Your new heart is a powerful, yet gentle, ruler. As you submit to God, the messages of your new heart will become so powerful that your body will divorce your brainwaves and begin to live with your new heart.

For example, if you read the scripture (outside information coming into your mind) that says, "Love thy neighbor as thyself," and your new heart (information from the heart of Christ) is already programmed to love your neighbor, when the evil thought arises to say, "Hate your neighbor," it will be ineffective.

Quench Not the Spirit

This is a list of human characteristics that can quench the action of the Holy Spirit in your life. Look up the Scripture passages in the other list, and match each trait with the scripture that describes it by writing the biblical citation in the blank.

- Greed _____   James 4:11

- Anger _____   John 14:27

- Selfish ambition _____   James 3:14–16

- Slander, being judgmental _____   James 1:20

- Anxiety, fear _____   Luke 12:15

What can you do when you realize that you've quenched the Spirit? (Read Romans 8:26–27; 2 Corinthians 7:9–11.)

_____

_____

_____

The message coming in that says "Love thy neighbor" combines with the new heart desire to love already inside of you and attacks that evil thought from both sides, squeezing it out.

When you disobey, the opposite happens. You can allow your brain's persistent resistance to prevail over the quiet intuitions of your new heart. We call this "quenching the Spirit."

Do not quench (suppress or subdue) the [Holy] Spirit.
—1 THESSALONIANS 5:19

As we read and obey His Word, everything hidden begins to be exposed. Your battle will be to submit to the Spirit's direction, and this can be an awesome fight. Your new heart will bring you to a valley of decision as you go through the process of purification.

GOD'S MEASURING LINE

God is the One who determines how well we are progressing in our transformation into the Christ-life after we receive our new hearts. When He brought His people out of captivity and returned them to the land of promise, He told them He was going to measure their progress on rebuilding His temple. "Therefore thus says the Lord: I have returned to Jerusalem with compassion (loving-kindness and mercy). My house shall be built in it, says the Lord of hosts, and a measuring line shall be stretched out over Jerusalem [with a view to rebuilding its walls]" (Zech. 1:16).

When God begins to restore and reconstruct the real temple within us, it will be done according to His measuring line, not our false weights and measures:

> So shall My word be that goes forth out of My mouth: it shall not return to Me void [without producing any effect, useless], but it shall accomplish that which I please and purpose, and it shall prosper in the thing for which I sent it. For you shall go out [from the spiritual exile caused by sin and evil into the homeland] with joy and be led forth [by your Leader, the Lord Himself, and His word] with peace; the mountains and the hills shall break forth before you into singing, and all the trees of the field shall clap their hands.
>
> —ISAIAH 55:11–12

God's Word will not return to Him empty. If we do not reject the new heart, the word God sends from His heart to ours will prosper. The words that come out of our mouths will reflect

His presence (just as they reflect His absence when we're living our old way). These words—not the empty confession from our brains—will yield eternal results, and our Father will be pleased. For "the good man brings good things out of the good stored up in his heart, and the evil man brings evil things out of the evil stored up in his heart. For out of the overflow of his heart his mouth speaks" (Luke 6:45, NIV).

> *For there is no good (healthy) tree that bears decayed (worthless, stale) fruit, nor on the other hand does a decayed (worthless, sickly) tree bear good fruit. For each tree is known and identified by its own fruit; for figs are not gathered from thornbushes, nor is a cluster of grapes picked from a bramblebush. The upright (honorable, intrinsically good) man out of the good treasure [stored] in his heart produces what is upright (honorable and intrinsically good), and the evil man out of the evil storehouse brings forth that which is depraved (wicked and intrinsically evil); for out of the abundance (overflow) of the heart his mouth speaks.*
>
> —LUKE 6:43–45

When we are doing well, He speaks directly to our new heart, saying, "Well done, good and faithful servant" (Matt. 25:23, KJV). God's voice is the only one that really counts.

Let us not think of ourselves more highly than we ought to think (Rom. 12:3). We can compliment each other, compare ourselves against one another, and say many things—but we must realize that many who encourage us are still "guppies" in the Spirit. (In the ocean, a guppy would be so tiny that it would say to a goldfish, "Oh, you are such a big, beautiful, bright fish!" A shark, on the other hand, would see things differently.)

We are utterly dependent upon God and the new heart that He puts within us. If we fail to trust and obey Him as He begins to purify our earthly temples, we can be taken prisoner again by the enemy. We can submit to God's rebuilding process, or we can go back to the pit. The choice is ours.

Memory Verse

By having the eyes of your heart flooded with light, so that you can know and understand the hope to which He has called you, and how rich is His glorious inheritance in the saints (His set-apart ones), and [so you can know and understand] what is the immeasurable and unlimited and surpassing greatness of His power in and for us who believe, as demonstrated in the working of His mighty strength.

—EPHESIANS 1:18–19

Heart to Heart

Dear heavenly Father:

Thank you for the gift of a new heart. I did not realize that my new heart would be in such conflict with my old behavior. These days, my mind and flesh have been warring against my new heart in the following ways:

_____

_____

Your gift to me is not only a new heart but also the complete guidance that I need to care for my new heart and to keep it beating with Your love. Today, please help me to replace_____

_____with_____

_____. I want to come one step closer to You. In Jesus' precious name, amen.

Just as the body of a heart transplant recipient tries to reject the new heart, so our flesh tries to reject the new heart.

CHAPTER 8

The New Heart

THE NEW HEART is an amazing mystery, and we must walk in the Spirit to understand its depths. We hold the feelings and purposes of God within us!

> For who has known or understood the mind (the counsels and purposes) of the Lord so as to guide and instruct Him and give Him knowledge? But we have the mind of Christ (the Messiah) and do hold the thoughts (feelings and purposes) of His heart.
> —1 CORINTHIANS 2:16

When you say, "I have been born again in Christ Jesus," the heart begins to function and rule. As I have said earlier, it has a lot of similarities with how our physical hearts function in our bodies.

And I will give them one heart [a new heart] and I will put a new spirit within them; and I will take the stony [unnaturally hardened] heart out of their flesh, and will give them a heart of flesh [sensitive and responsive to the touch of their God], that they may walk in My statutes and keep My ordinances, and do them. And they shall be My people, and I will be their God.
—EZEKIEL 11:19–20

THE ATMOSPHERE OF THE NEW HEART

By the twenty-fifth day of a woman's pregnancy, her baby's heart has formed and started its rhythm. Through its beating, it pumps blood through the arteries and veins, providing oxygen, nutrients, cleansing, and energy for every part of the body.

Your new spiritual heart is also able to send "waves" of life, quickening your brain and the rest of your being to the ways of God.

> But if the Spirit of him that raised up Jesus from the dead dwell in you, he that raised up Christ from the dead shall also quicken your mortal bodies by his Spirit that dwelleth in you.
>
> —ROMANS 8:11, KJV

Babies are comforted by the sound of a mother's heartbeat. In his book *The Heart's Code*, Paul Pearsall mentions one experiment where, when nurses played a recorded heartbeat in a hospital nursery, the crying of the newborn babies was reduced by more than 50 percent.

Our new hearts are comforted and helped when they "hear God's heartbeat." In an atmosphere of worship, they are reminded of their heavenly home, and they are restored to a state of balance and harmony.

When a baby is delivered out of its mother's womb, the nurses wrap the baby up and hand it to the mother, who holds her baby close to her heart. This makes the newborn feel warm and protected, just as it was in the womb. In the same way, we need to be wrapped in an atmosphere of worship and held where we can hear God's heartbeat. Just as a baby enjoys "womb-like" conditions after birth, so the new heart hungers and thirsts after righteousness and thrives in the atmosphere of worship, which reminds it of heaven.

Your new heart desires the things of God above the things of this world. You will find yourself saying, "I have to wash dishes,

Guard Your Heart

Most of us are careless with our hearts. We choose "food" that is ungodly, neglect to "exercise" our heart in worship, take our heart for granted, fail to listen to our heart, and so on.

1. What makes you neglect your heart? Anxiety? Fatigue? Pride? Temptations to sin?

_____

_____

2. How can you tell when your heart has been neglected?

_____

_____

3. What does your heart need right now? Has it been neglected? Pause for a moment of listening prayer. What does God's Spirit tell you that your heart needs?

_____

_____

4. Pause again and prayerfully ask Him to furnish what you need.

but I feel like glorifying God!" No longer will you think, *Oh, no, I have to pray,* or *I have to go to church.* Instead, you will think, *I have to go to work, but I want to stay here in His presence!*

Your new heart will no longer sit in your pew at church and have to be forced to worship! No longer will you watch the clock as you hurriedly take three minutes to pray as your day begins. No longer will you have to deal with feelings of dislike or hatred toward your fellow man; your new heart will compel you to love others.

This heart is bursting with the characteristics of Christ and longs for opportunities to express Christ through your actions. To keep your new heart healthy and strong, you have to keep it in the atmosphere of the Spirit. It was born in the Spirit realm.

> *My son, attend to my words; consent and submit to my sayings. Let them not depart from your sight; keep them in the center of your heart. For they are life to those who find them, healing and health to all their flesh. Keep and guard your heart with all vigilance and above all that you guard, for out of it flow the springs of life.*
> —PROVERBS 4:20–23

RESPONDING TO THE RHYTHMS OF THE NEW HEART

Just as your physical heart influences the autonomic (subconscious, automatic) functions of your body (like breathing, for example), your new heart will gently begin to influence your behavior. You will desire to do something that will please God, sometimes even before you have learned the Scriptures, which tell you that is what you should do!

> But as for you, the anointing (the sacred appointment, the unction) which you received from Him abides [permanently] in you; [so] then you have no need that anyone should instruct you. But just as His anointing teaches you concerning everything and is true and is no falsehood, so you must abide in (live in, never depart from) Him [being rooted in Him, knit to Him], just as [His anointing] has taught you [to do].
> —1 JOHN 2:27

I have seen people who were converted who did not know the first thing about God before their conversion. They had not been raised in the church. After their conversion they started saying things like, "He told me to turn that movie off." "He told me not to wear that because it was too seductive." "He told me to take the earring out of my lip."

I would ask, "You found that in the Scriptures?"

They would reply, "No, I have not read about it, but that is what God told me to do." What they were doing is responding automatically to the new information flowing out of their new hearts. They were obeying the gentle promptings of Almighty God.

When we obey His promptings instead of the old promptings of the flesh, we begin to grow in the fruit of the Spirit:

> But the fruit of the [Holy] Spirit [the work which His presence within accomplishes] is love, joy (gladness), peace, patience (an even temper, forbearance), kindness, goodness (benevolence), faithfulness, gentleness (meekness, humility), self-control (self-restraint, continence).
>
> —GALATIANS 5:22–23

Instead of ignoring our consciences, we begin to listen to the intelligent language of our new hearts. (The Scriptures tell us repeatedly to "hearken" unto the Word of the Lord. In the Hebrew, this word means "to hear intelligently." See Leviticus 26; Deuteronomy 15:5; 1 Kings 11:38; Proverbs 8:32; Isaiah 46:12.)

Therefore if any person is [ingrafted] in Christ (the Messiah) he is a new creation (a new creature altogether); the old [previous moral and spiritual condition] has passed away. Behold, the fresh and new has come!
—2 CORINTHIANS 5:17

Remade in His Image

God created men and women "in His own image" (Gen. 1:27). But sin soon corrupted that image. When you surrender your old, corrupted heart and receive a new, pure heart, God restores you so that you are remade in His image.

Next to the scriptures quoted below, write either "God" or "Me" to indicate which party takes the initiative in each case:

"So God created man in his own image, in the image of God he created him; male and female he created them" (Gen. 1:27, NIV). _____

"For God, who said, 'Let light shine out of darkness,' made his light shine in our hearts to give us the light of the knowledge of the glory of God in the face of Christ" (2 Cor. 4:6, NIV). _____

"You were taught, with regard to your former way of life, to put off your old self, which is being corrupted by its deceitful desires; to be made new in the attitude of your minds; and to put on the new self, created to be like God in true righteousness and holiness" (Eph. 4:22–24, NIV). _____

"Be imitators of God, therefore, as dearly loved children and live a life of love, just as Christ loved us and gave himself up for us as a fragrant offering and sacrifice to God" (Eph. 5:1–2, NIV). _____

Can your new heart be corrupted? (See Hebrews 3:12–14.)

_____

Read Hebrews 10:22–25. List several ways you can take action to keep your new heart pure:

_____

_____

_____

_____

_____

_____

Getting Personal

I have been growing in my walk with Christ for several years. Recently I went back to my old neighborhood where somebody commented that I had really changed. That caused me to take stock of myself.

Here are some of the marks of God's healing and retraining work that I can see: In general, I am much more contented. I'm losing my ability to worry, and I'm much less "committed" to my moods. I'm not as bothered by other people—somehow I can love them in spite of their actions. I think I'm friendlier with strangers and much quicker to show affection to my loved ones. I didn't touch people, and now I notice that I reach out to them all the time. I notice that I like to read Scripture more. (Sometimes when I have an extra minute, I just pick up the Bible and start to read.) Here's another one: I don't talk to myself as much! I used to have all these long, useless mental conversations. Now my emotions are more stable and my thinking processes are clearer. As a result, I can more quickly figure out whether something is from my old way of thinking or from the devil—or from God. I'm glad about these changes. In fact, I'm *very* grateful. God is so good!

—*B. D.*

ONLY THE BLOOD CAN SAVE US

Just as the heart that beats in your chest cavity needs blood to survive, and "blood is the heart's business" as it is pumped to the rest of your body, so the blood of Jesus keeps your new heart alive and your new heart pumps Jesus' blood to every part of your body.

And just as a heart transplant patient must receive life-giving blood transfusions as a part of the transplant process, so when you receive a new heart, you have also received new blood—Christ's blood! This new blood is how the new heart stays purified, because the blood of Jesus washes away your sin and brings life.

This new blood identifies you with the Father and sets the atmosphere for the new heart. When we are born again and receive a new heart, the spiritual "DNA" in our blood is new, and it matches Jesus and His Father. We become God's sons and daughters, which causes us to become more like Him as we obey our new heart. You know that DNA always reveals who the real father is!

But now in Christ Jesus, you who once were [so] far away, through (by, in) the blood of Christ have been brought near.

—EPHESIANS 2:13

Jesus' Blood

Christians can talk too lightly about "Jesus' blood," and the words can become meaningless. What is the significance of Jesus' blood?

Read the following three scriptures, first from the Old Testament, where God laid out His requirements for His people, and then from the New Testament, where He explained how Jesus fulfilled those requirements:

For the life (the animal soul) is in the blood, and I have given it for you upon the altar to make atonement for your souls; for it is the blood that makes atonement, by reason of the life [which it represents].

—LEVITICUS 17:11

[In fact] under the Law almost everything is purified by means of blood, and without the shedding there is neither release from sin and its guilt nor the remission of the due and merited punishment for sins.

—HEBREWS 9:22

In this the love of God was made manifest (displayed) where we are concerned: in that God sent His Son, the only begotten or unique [Son], into the world so that we might live through Him. In this is love: not that we loved God, but that He loved us and sent His Son to be the propitiation (the atoning sacrifice) for our sins.

—1 JOHN 4:9–10

1. When an animal was sacrificed, did it survive the experience?

_____

Could the sacrificial blood be obtained by merely injuring the animal?

_____

_____

2. "The next day John saw Jesus coming toward him and said, 'Look, the Lamb of God, who takes away the sin of the world!'" (John 1:29, NIV). Why is Jesus called the "Lamb of God"? (See also Leviticus 5:5–6.)

_____

_____

_____

3. How is the Lamb of God associated with the idea of shedding blood?

_____

_____

_____

4. In one word, *why* did God send Jesus to die? What was His motivation? (See John 3:16.)

_____

5. "God presented him [Jesus] as a sacrifice of atonement" (Rom. 3:25, NIV). The word *atonement* means "a making at one," or "at-one-ment." Who was to become one with whom?

_____

_____

6. In other words, for whom did God offer Jesus as a sacrifice? (See Romans 8:32.)

_____

7. What significance does this have for you personally?

_____

_____

How much more surely shall the blood of Christ, Who by virtue of [His] eternal Spirit [His own preexistent divine personality] has offered Himself as an unblemished sacrifice to God, purify our consciences from dead works and lifeless observances to serve the [ever] living God?

—HEBREWS 9:14

THE HEART CRY OF GOD

Your new heart is the heart of God. It comes with His will, His ways, His purpose, His assignment, and His obedience. This heart, and only this heart, contains the power to change the way you live.

So ask yourself these questions: "Am I really saved? Though I cried on the altar, did I really get converted? Though I am in church, faithful to attend services, sitting on the second pew every Sunday, has my heart been changed? Did I really receive a heart transplant from God? Do I really have the new heart?"

Memory Verse

To Him Who ever loves us and has once [for all] loosed and freed us from our sins by His own blood, and formed us into a kingdom (a royal race), priests to His God and Father—to Him be the glory and the power and the majesty and the dominion throughout the ages and forever and ever. Amen (so be it).
—Revelation 1:5–6

Heart to Heart

I say to you, Ask and keep on asking and it shall be given you; seek and keep on seeking and you shall find; knock and keep on knocking and the door shall be opened to you. For everyone who asks and keeps on asking receives; and he who seeks and keeps on seeking finds; and to him who knocks and keeps on knocking, the door shall be opened" (Luke 11:9–10).

Dear Father,

Do I have the new heart You have prepared for me? Has my old diseased heart been replaced with the one transplanted from Your Son? Is His cleansing blood circulating inside of me? I will wait silently before You and expect You to speak to my heart. [If you seek answers to these questions, you will find them. Write below what God says to you in response to your questions:]

_____

_____

_____

 HEART BEAT HEART BEAT HEART BEAT

The new heart is your vital connection with the ways of heaven, and it pumps the cleansing blood of Jesus so that your spiritual life is sustained.

CHAPTER 9

The Renewed Mind

A NEW HEART is the deposit, or assurance, from God that He is also going to make your mind new. Although you get a new heart at once, your mind must be transformed in stages and in levels. As Christians, our daily battleground is the progressive renewing of our minds. We must let the Word pierce each part of our minds, transforming our thoughts and emotions on both the subconscious and conscious levels.

> *For the Word that God speaks is alive and full of power [making it active, operative, energizing, and effective]; it is sharper than any two-edged sword, penetrating to the dividing line of the breath of life (soul) and [the immortal] spirit, and of joints and marrow [of the deepest parts of our nature], exposing and sifting and analyzing and judging the very thoughts and purposes of the heart.*
>
> —HEBREWS 4:12

LEVELS OF CONSCIOUSNESS PENETRATED BY TRUTH

Electroencephalograms (EEGs) measure brain activity. Ranked in the order of wave cycles per second, EEGs measure Delta, Theta, Alpha, and Beta waves. Delta and Theta waves can be measured when we are sleeping (and in children when awake), whereas Alpha and Beta waves characterize our awake (conscious) state.

God uses your new heart to influence your brainwaves. Progressively, He will transform you into His image in the way you think and consequently in the way you act. Even without comprehending the complexities of the human brain, we can recognize that our minds—whether they are sluggish or hyperactive, over- or under-influenced by our emotions and our consciences—cannot be transformed by our own efforts. They need to come under the lordship of Jesus Christ.

God could not establish a covenant relationship with us through our brains, so He has chosen to rule in our lives through our new hearts. When this new heart from God begins to govern us, we begin to see with a new perspective, even if we do not understand why. Without the governing influence of the new heart, we can fall prey to negative emotions like fear, anger, blame, or insecurity. But with a new heart, we begin to respond in new ways. The more we cooperate with God's signals, the more our minds are renewed.

The substance of your new heart is Truth, so your new heart reveals the truth around you. That is why you can look at something that Satan has camouflaged to look like God and call it a lie. You are also able to look at something that has the "form of godliness" and know that there is no truth in it and that eternal love does not live there. Jesus said, "You will know the truth, and the truth will set you free" (John 8:32, NIV).

Your new heart is already equipped with the ability to believe God. It comes "built with faith." Your mind must learn to demonstrate, on every level, what the heart believes. A powerful confidence flows out of the new heart, a confidence Jesus demonstrated when He came into the world.

Jesus said confidently, "I am the door…I am the way…I am the resurrection." He did not say, "I *think* I am the door…I *think* I am the way…I *think* I am the resurrection." And if Jesus Christ, indeed, is the Word "made flesh" that has dwelled among us—and now the Word lives inside of us—we can now make our confessions with assurance. Confidently we can declare, "I am healed; I am delivered; I am set free!"

If then you have been raised with Christ [to a new life, thus sharing His resurrection from the dead], aim at and seek the [rich, eternal treasures] that are above, where Christ is, seated at the right hand of God. And set your minds and keep them set on what is above (the higher things), not on the things that are on the earth. For [as far as this world is concerned] you have died, and your [new, real] life is hidden with Christ in God.

—Colossians 3:1–3

Transformed

Do not be conformed to this world (this age), [fashioned after and adapted to its external, superficial customs], but be transformed (changed) by the [entire] renewal of your mind [by its new ideals and its new attitude], so that you may prove [for yourselves] what is the good and acceptable and perfect will of God, even the thing which is good and acceptable and perfect [in His sight for you].

—Romans 12:2

1. "Be transformed (changed) by the [entire] renewal of your mind...." Is this a one-time-event or a process?

_____

2. "Be transformed...." Is Paul making merely a strong suggestion in this verse—or is it a command?

_____

3. Do you undertake this transformation as an active participant or as a passive one? (See Ephesians 4:22–24.)

_____

4. What are some of the negative consequences if you ignore this part of the salvation process? (See 1 John 2:15–17; James 4:4–8; Hebrews 12:27.)

_____

_____

_____

_____

5. What are some of the positive consequences if you allow yourself to be transformed? (See the same three scriptures: 1 John 2:15–17; James 4:4–8; Hebrews 12:27.)

_____

_____

_____

_____

6. List some of the practical actions involved in this transformation process. (See Colossians 3; Ephesians 5 and 6; Titus 3:9–11.) What do you "put off" and what do you "put on"?

_____

_____

_____

_____

_____

_____

WHY DIDN'T I THINK?

So often we say and do things before we realize why we have said them. We react, and then we think.

As our new hearts begin to rule and our minds are renewed, we will notice that even our reactions are different. With your old heart, you might slap somebody who offends you. With your transplanted heart from God, your first response should be, *What would God do?* Someone might ask you, "Why didn't you slap her? Why didn't you cuss her out?"

Standing there (with the heart of God) you would say, "I could not open my mouth. The Holy Spirit would not let me say a word." Out of the abundance of your (new) heart come your speech patterns and your reactions. (See Matthew 12:34.)

I know this is true from my own experiences. God has put me in predicaments where I knew I should have gone off about something, yet He would not let me open my mouth. I knew that I had been wronged, but God still led me to bless the people who wronged me.

And I am convinced and sure of this very thing, that He Who began a good work in you will continue until the day of Jesus Christ [right up to the time of His return], developing [that good work] and perfecting and bringing it to full completion in you. It is right and appropriate for me to have this confidence and feel this way about you all, because you have me in your heart and I hold you in my heart as partakers and sharers, one and all with me, of grace (God's unmerited favor and spiritual blessing)....

And this I pray: that your love may abound yet more and more and extend to its fullest development in knowledge and all keen insight [that your love may display itself in greater depth of acquaintance and more comprehensive discernment], so that you may surely learn to sense what is vital, and approve and prize what is excellent and of real value [recognizing the highest and the best, and distinguishing the moral differences], and that you may be untainted and pure and unerring and blameless [so that with hearts sincere and certain and unsullied, you may approach] the day of Christ [not stumbling nor causing others to stumble]. May you abound in and be filled with the fruits of righteousness (of right standing with God and right doing) which come through Jesus Christ (the Anointed One), to the honor and praise of God [that His glory may be both manifested and recognized].

—PHILIPPIANS 1:6–7, 9–11

THE MIND/BODY CONNECTION

The second chapter of 1 Corinthians gives an awesome understanding of the mind/body connection. The apostle Paul was a highly educated man. Yet as he begins this chapter, he clearly states that he was determined that his new heart would not be reconnected to his philosophy or to anything that he had studied in the past. He opted for a permanent disconnection!

As for myself, brethren, when I came to you, I did not come proclaiming to you the testimony and evidence or mystery and secret of God [concerning what He has done through Christ for the salvation of men] in lofty words of eloquence or human philosophy and wisdom. For I resolved to know nothing (to be acquainted with nothing, to make a display of the knowledge of nothing, and to be conscious of nothing) among you except Jesus Christ (the Messiah) and Him crucified.

—1 CORINTHIANS 2:1–2

In verses 4 through 7, Paul teaches us about heart wisdom—something very different from the knowledge from the mind. It is

Getting Personal

It's wonderful when one of God's tests shows you that you have changed, deep down inside.

After I had been a Christian for a few years, my husband suddenly became very sick. He was taken to the hospital, and I was following in our car after getting a friend to come over to look after my two babies. I was so scared. My heart was racing. However, much to my surprise, my mind was clear and my heart was full of faith. (I didn't realize that would be my automatic response until the crisis hit.) I did not panic. I did not rush frantically. I made sure my friend knew what to do for my children. I remembered the names of certain people who could help me legally and financially if my husband should die or be debilitated. And I decided—with a kind of fierce joy—that I would drive away the devil by launching into loud worship as I drove to the emergency room. When I got there, I was so peaceful that it must have showed. The doctors even let me stay in the examining room when they did a spinal tap on my husband, although usually they ask family members to leave the room.

It turned out that my husband didn't die, but we had a long recovery ahead. Now I knew I had a firm foundation of real faith inside, and I was that much less likely to react in old ways to the stresses and strains of life.

Of course, some negative things tended to rise up inside me as his recovery wore me out. But I found that it really works to "take every thought captive" to Jesus. I love the freedom of maturity in Christ! I praise God for allowing us to grow up in Him, and I don't ever want to take it for granted.

—K. R.

a wisdom available only to those who have received a new heart. Paul describes this experience by saying:

> My language and my message were not set forth in persuasive (enticing and plausible) words of wisdom, but they were in demonstration of the [Holy] Spirit and power [a proof by the Spirit and power of God, operating on me and stirring in the minds of my hearers the most holy emotions and thus persuading them], so that your faith might not rest in the wisdom of men (human philosophy), but in the power of God.
>
> Yet when we are among the full-grown (spiritually mature Christians who are ripe in understanding), we

do impart a [higher] wisdom (the knowledge of the divine plan previously hidden); but it is indeed not a wisdom of this present age or of this world nor of the leaders and rulers of this age, who are being brought to nothing and are doomed to pass away.

But rather what we are setting forth is a wisdom of God once hidden [from the human understanding] and now revealed to us by God—[that wisdom] which God devised and decreed before the ages for our glorification [to lift us into the glory of His presence].

—1 CORINTHIANS 2:4–7

My message and my preaching were not with wise and persuasive words, but with a demonstration of the Spirit's power, so that your faith might not rest on men's wisdom, but on God's power.

We do, however, speak a message of wisdom among the mature, but not the wisdom of this age or of the rulers of this age, who are coming to nothing. No, we speak of God's secret wisdom, a wisdom that has been hidden and that God destined for our glory before time began.

—1 CORINTHIANS 2:4–7, NIV

Through Paul, God is teaching us that we cannot grab hold of God—or of the knowledge and wisdom that is God's alone—with our natural minds. To understand God, we must receive the new heart.

Wisdom from God

Who is wise and understanding among you? Let him show it by his good life, by deeds done in the humility that comes from wisdom. But if you harbor bitter envy and selfish ambition in your hearts, do not boast about it or deny the truth. Such "wisdom" does not come down from heaven but is earthly, unspiritual, of the devil. For where you have envy and selfish ambition, there you find disorder and every evil practice. But the wisdom that comes from heaven is first of all pure; then peace-loving, considerate, submissive, full of mercy and good fruit, impartial and sincere.

—JAMES 3:13–17, NIV

1. Based on these verses from the Book of James, list several characteristics of the so-called wisdom that does *not* come from God:

_____

_____

_____

2. Where does this so-called wisdom come from?

_____

3. List several unmistakable evidences of the wisdom of God in a person's life.

_____

_____

_____

4. Read Ephesians 5:13–6:9. As you read, look for the specifics of Paul's advice regarding human relationships with others. For each type of relationship, what evidences of wise thinking and holy living does he hope to see?

• "One another" (the church, fellow believers)

_____

_____

_____

- Wives

- Husbands

- Children

- Fathers

- "Slaves" (workers, employees)

- "Masters" (supervisors, employers)

5. Which categories do you fit into?

6. From the evidence you find in Scripture, would you say that God's wisdom is:
   a. Philosophical, "ivory tower" quality, or
   b. Quality that has down-to-earth, practical applications?

Support your answer with at least two Scripture references:

EVIDENCE THAT WE HAVE A NEW HEART

Paul helps us to recognize the evidence that we have received a new heart and that we possess the heart wisdom about which he speaks in the second chapter of 1 Corinthians. It is like growing from infancy to adulthood. (See 1 Corinthians 3:1–3.)

As we grow, God will test us to see if our character is being built on the foundation of a new heart.

> But if anyone builds upon the Foundation, whether it be with gold, silver, precious stones, wood, hay, straw, the work of each [one] will become [plainly, openly] known (shown for what it is); for the day [of Christ] will disclose and declare it, because it will be revealed with fire, and the fire will test and critically appraise the character and worth of the work each person has done.
>
> —1 Corinthians 3:12–13

The fire or testing will reveal whether your heart is made of gold, silver, and precious stones (the new heart) or if it is composed of hay, wood, stubble, or straw (the old heart). We will be tested in the fire of our daily living. The enemy will throw his fiery darts at us.

But the fire does not come to harm us—it comes to appraise us. It is in the crucible of God's fire of testing that the evidence of our new heart begins to shine forth. It is as though God is saying, "Just checking. Just checking to see if My heart is still in there. Just checking to see if My blood is still running through your veins."

Therefore, my dear ones, as you have always obeyed [my suggestions], so now, not only [with the enthusiasm you would show] in my presence but much more because I am absent, work out (cultivate, carry out to the goal, and fully complete) your own salvation with reverence and awe and trembling (self-distrust, with serious caution, tenderness of conscience, watchfulness against temptation, timidly shrinking from whatever might offend God and discredit the name of Christ). [Not in your own strength] for it is God Who is all the while effectually at work in you [energizing and creating in you the power and desire], both to will and to work for His good pleasure and satisfaction and delight.

—PHILIPPIANS 2:12–13

What Does the Evidence Show?

To help you take stock of your own life, use a number scale to rank yourself on the questions below. Try *not* to compare yourself to other people, and don't compare yourself to an impossible standard of perfection. Start by choosing a point in time in the past (a few years ago, perhaps, or whenever you surrendered your heart to Jesus), and let that time be represented by the zero. How have you changed since then?

1.   How am I doing in my moral conduct, including my thoughts? (Am I living by biblical standards of honesty and purity? Can I respond to the conviction of the Spirit? Am I able to depend on the Spirit for help?)

-3	-2	-1	0	+1	+2	+3
Destitute	Feeble	Uninspired		Changing	Improving	Renewed

2.   How am I doing in my relationships? (Am I learning to live in peace? Am I learning to resolve differences in a godly way? Are people noticing a difference?)

-3	-2	-1	0	+1	+2	+3
Destitute	Feeble	Uninspired		Changing	Improving	Renewed

3.   How am I doing in my speech? (Am I refraining from gossip, slander, and unclean speech? Do I speak words of encouragement and faith?)

-3	-2	-1	0	+1	+2	+3
Destitute	Feeble	Uninspired		Changing	Improving	Renewed

4. How am I doing with my finances and possessions? (Do I tend to worry about them? Do I envy others who have more? Do I help others with my money and property?)

-3	-2	-1	0	+1	+2	+3
Destitute	Feeble	Uninspired		Changing	Improving	Renewed

5. How am I doing regarding my circumstances? (Am I learning to rejoice regardless of what is happening? Am I trusting God?)

-3	-2	-1	0	+1	+2	+3
Destitute	Feeble	Uninspired		Changing	Improving	Renewed

6. How am I doing as a member of the church? (Have I been giving my time and money to build the body of Christ? Are my spiritual gifts bearing fruit?)

-3	-2	-1	0	+1	+2	+3
Destitute	Feeble	Uninspired		Changing	Improving	Renewed

7. How does my "public self" compare with my "private self"? (If someone could read my mind or watch me when I'm alone, would I be ashamed? Do I sometimes do good deeds that no one ever knows about?)

-3	-2	-1	0	+1	+2	+3
Destitute	Feeble	Uninspired		Changing	Improving	Renewed

8. How am I doing in being faithful to my commitments? (Do I follow through on my promises? Are other people able to depend on me?)

-3	-2	-1	0	+1	+2	+3
Destitute	Feeble	Uninspired		Changing	Improving	Renewed

9. What can you do about the areas where you see the need for improvement?

MEDITATION AND RENEWAL

Your word have I laid up in my heart, that I might not
sin against You.

—PSALM 119:11

As you keep putting God's Word inside of you, it will change your thinking on all levels. The Word itself speaks of this changed, renewed thinking. In Romans 12:2, Paul wrote, "Do not be conformed to this world...but be transformed (changed) by the [entire] renewal of your mind [by its new ideals and its new attitude], so that you may prove [for yourselves] what is the good and acceptable and perfect will of God."

I believe that when you receive the new heart, its power breaks the shackles of things that possessed you as a sinner. Even though there are still things that you love and do not want to release, your renewed mind can give power to your decision to surrender those things to the Lord.

Step by step, your mind is changed and your life renewed.

Memory Verse   *And be not conformed to this world: but be ye transformed by the renewing of your mind, that ye may prove what is that good, and acceptable, and perfect, will of God.*
—ROMANS 12:2, KJV

Heart to Heart

The first three sentences of this prayer are drawn straight from the three verses in the Psalms (Ps. 119:11, 32; 19:14, NIV). Find a verse or two in another psalm (or more than one) that can help you speak from your heart to God's heart:

Jesus, my Lord, I have hidden Your Word in my heart that I might not sin against You....I run in the path of Your commands, for You have set my heart free....May the words of my mouth and the meditation of my heart be pleasing in Your sight, O Lord, my Rock and my Redeemer.

_____

_____

_____

_____

_____

Amen.

 HEART B EAT HEART B EAT HEART B EAT

The new heart makes it possible for you to have a renewed mind.

CHAPTER 10

Rejection of the New Heart

IF YOU END up continuing in a pattern of sin, you have not received the new heart. Many people, even in the church, live in a perpetual state of sin, saying, "I do not feel convicted about this. I do not feel bad about that." Their consciences have become darkened, and they habitually do things that displease God. If you do not love God or fear Him "unto obedience," you do not have the new heart.

THE DANGER OF HABITUAL SIN

If you persistently do ungodly things and sense no conviction (telling yourself, "God understands"), your old heart has deceived you. You are walking out a death sentence. When you reject the Word and do not put it into your heart and mind, the old nature assumes control—and you shut down the power and the activity of your new heart. God will not stay in this temple.

Anyone can make a mistake. Falling into temptation and sin does not mean that you are doomed. But when ungodly behavior becomes habitual to the point that you no longer sense the heart's conviction, the new heart has been repelled. Because you have ignored the new heart's correction—deliberately annihilating its message, which says that you no longer desire God—you have rejected your new heart. To consistently refuse the direction of the new heart sends a signal back to it: "I do not want you here." The Spirit of the Lord will never stay where He is not wanted.

Getting Personal

I am learning how to look after my new heart, which is another way of saying I'm trying to be obedient to God.

I have discovered that there's something beautiful in repentance. I have begun to appreciate even my bad moments, because they show me that I need to step up my efforts. There's no use putting up a façade to hide things like anxiety or anger or bitterness. Those things will tend to show via trouble in my relationships, grumbling, even indigestion and insomnia.

Once I heard a children's pastor explain it this way: It's like God is holding each of us from heaven with a string. When we sin, we cut the string and fall. But if we look back to God, it's like God ties it up again. And you know what happens when you tie together two pieces of string—it gets shorter. So we're closer to Him every time we repent and He forgives us.

—G. P.

When you have a new heart—God's heart—and you do anything that is contrary to God's Word, it will automatically send a wave of conviction. And because you love and fear God and believe in His name, you will repent.

God's new heart comes with divine passion for the things of the Spirit. The new heart craves what God craves, loves what He loves, and hates what He hates. So how is it that we can say we have received the heart of God if we do *not* love what He loves, hate what He hates, or crave after His righteousness?

When we receive God's heart, it should birth within us a passion for holiness, worship, and everything that pleases Him. It should automatically reject anything that does not sound, look, taste, or feel like God. If it does not do this, something is wrong. Unless we train our minds (and, as a result, our flesh) to line up with our new hearts, we will fall into deception.

This is how a person falls into a backslidden state. The new heart says, "Do not do this." But the mind refuses over and over again, saying, "I am going to do what I want."

Danger!

Is it really true that you can lose the faith-filled heart that God gives you? Where in Scripture does He warn us about this? Read Romans 11:22; 1 Corinthians 15:2; Colossians 1:22–23; Hebrews 3:6.

Each one of these verses contains a "qualifier," a phrase that makes the truth of the rest of the sentence applicable only if certain conditions are met. Blessings will belong to believers *if* they do something. For example, in Romans 11:22, we read, "Note and appreciate the gracious kindness...of God." But His kindness applies to your life *only* "provided that you continue in His grace and abide in His kindness."

1. What are the "qualifiers" in the other verses in the list?

    1 Corinthians 15:2 _____

    Colossians 1:22–23 _____

    Hebrews 3:6 _____

2. What are the blessings offered to us in these same verses?

    1 Corinthians 15:2 _____

    Colossians 1:22–23 _____

    Hebrews 3:6 _____

3. What does it mean to "continue in His grace and abide in His kindness"?

    Romans 11:22 (See also Romans 2:4.) _____

    _____

4. In your own words, sum up the main idea expressed in these verses. How would you sum it up if you were writing it in a letter to a new believer?

    _____

    _____

    _____

    _____

> *Then note and appreciate the gracious kindness and the severity*
> *of God: severity toward those who have fallen, but God's gracious*
> *kindness to you—provided you continue in His grace and abide in*
> *His kindness; otherwise you too will be cut off (pruned away).*
>
> —ROMANS 11:22

OVERTAKEN IN SIN, OR A REPROBATE MIND?

If you allow your flesh (mind) to lead you into sin, and then you repent, God will forgive you. You have been overtaken in a fault that cropped up from your mind. God knows that your motivation to sin did not come from your heart. In fact, it was your heart that convicted you and sent you running to Him for forgiveness.

But if you persist in sinning, God will allow your sin to prevail.

> And so, since they did not see fit to acknowledge God
> or approve of Him or consider Him worth the knowing,
> God gave them over to a base and condemned mind to
> do things not proper or decent but loathsome.
>
> —ROMANS 1:28

When God turns someone over to a "reprobate mind," more often than not it is someone who has declared that he has a new heart. Although that person has received convicting messages from God, he ignores them—continuously. His actions become a mockery against God. God has no other choice but to turn that person over to a reprobate mind.

This is the danger that faces the church today. Many people are saying, "I am saved," as they willfully and continually do things that displease God. That offends Him, to the point that He turns them over to their deceived and debased minds.

It would be better for these people to say, "I was saved, but I am in a backslidden state right now. I need prayer. My thoughts are too strong. I cannot overthrow them." There is grace and mercy for these individuals. But when they constantly reject the waves of conviction from their new hearts, declaring how righteous and holy they are, the Spirit of the Lord will leave them.

> For if anyone only listens to the Word without obeying it and being a doer of it, he is like a man who looks carefully at his [own] natural face in a mirror; for he thoughtfully observes himself, and then goes off and promptly forgets what he is like.
>
> —James 1:23–24

They are committing spiritual suicide by putting to death the breath of life that God has placed in their hearts. They know the truth, but over and over again they reject it. Then they walk away and pretend that everything is OK. This leaves God with no alternative.

If we deliberately keep on sinning after we have received the knowledge of the truth, no sacrifice for sins is left, but only a fearful expectation of judgment and of raging fire that will consume the enemies of God. Anyone who rejected the law of Moses died without mercy on the testimony of two or three witnesses. How much more severely do you think a man deserves to be punished who has trampled the Son of God under foot, who has treated as an unholy thing the blood of the covenant that sanctified him, and who has insulted the Spirit of grace?... It is a dreadful thing to fall into the hands of the living God.

—Hebrews 10:26–29, 31, niv

God's Judgment

We don't like to think about God's judgment. In fact, many people deny the truth of it. This denial could be dangerous to their eternal welfare.

Read Hebrews 10:26–31.

1. What kind of people is this text referring to—believers or unbelievers?

_____

2. What is the underlying attitude of those who "deliberately keep on sinning"?

_____

_____

3. What is the ordinary remedy for sin? (See Romans 10:13; Acts 4:12.)

_____

4. Why does that remedy not apply in this situation? (See Hebrews 6:4–8.)

_____

_____

5. What is your protection against the influence of "reprobates"? (See Jude 20–21.)

_____

_____

THE NEW EVIL HEART

God cannot dwell in the same place as sin. When you backslide, your latter state becomes worse than your original state before receiving the new heart. If God has given you a new heart to replace your old one, yet you reject that new heart, you will not merely revert back to the old heart you had before. You will receive another heart from Satan, one that is prepared to receive seven times the amount of evil that you once held in your old heart.

When you "rend your heart" (Joel 2:13) and give it to God, do you think that He puts it in a bank account to save it? Do you think that He puts it into cold storage, saying, "I will save it just in case you do not want Me later?" No! He destroys it. Since He came to give us everlasting, abundant life, He destroys anything that resembles death.

When a surgeon takes out an old, damaged heart, he does not try to restore it. He discards it. Then if your body rejects your new heart, the doctors would never go back and get your old one. They couldn't—it is gone! So they would put your name back on the list to receive a second new heart, and you would have to wait for another donor. Spiritually, you don't want your next donor to be Satan.

If you reject your new heart from God, Satan brings you an evil heart, and that heart looks like it is in perfect order—until it begins its evil transformation.

For if, after they have escaped the pollutions of the world through [the full, personal] knowledge of our Lord and Savior Jesus Christ, they again become entangled in them and are overcome, their last condition is worse [for them] than the first.

—2 PETER 2:20

This ought to make you hold on to God even if you have to fight tooth and nail. This knowledge should make you determined to put your old mind to death. It should make you feed your mind with the Word of God every day, because you do not ever want to backslide.

Avoiding Traps

Read Hebrews 3:7–11. The writer is quoting Psalm 95:7–11.

1. Who is speaking these words (Heb. 3:7)?

_____

2. What group of people was tested in the desert for forty years?

_____

3. What was the condition of their hearts? (v. 8)

_____

4. God is not passive in the face of persistent sin. He denies persistent sinners access to the blessings they could have had if they had lived in a way that pleased Him. Look up Romans 14:23. Below, copy the last part of the verse, which is a good definition of sin.

_____

_____

_____

5. How did the Israelites sin (Heb. 3:8–10)?

_____

_____

_____

6. How can we follow the advice (v. 8), "Do not harden your hearts..."?

_____

_____

_____

_____

THE TIME FOR CHANGE HAS COME

At one time, my pastor was eating things that were unhealthy for his body. The artery leading to his heart became clogged because of things he had eaten (that his mind had told him he should have). This was not his heart's desire. His mind had said, "I want bacon." Did his heart completely fail him? No, he had a stroke, so there was nothing wrong with his heart. Yet there was something wrong with the artery that led to his heart.

When people fall into temptation, it does not necessarily mean their hearts are messed up. They may have had a spiritual stroke. The "artery" can be unclogged through spiritual surgery according to the Word of God so that the blood can continue to flow to the heart and brain.

When a doctor tells his patient what to do in order to stay healthy, and she refuses to obey his orders, eating everything that she can get her hands on, it will ultimately affect her heart. If she has a stroke, she can become paralyzed and possibly lose the ability to think clearly, move, or talk. Her body and face could become twisted and distorted. On the spiritual side, this would mean she would no longer resemble Christ. Her heart would still be in intact, but the stroke would indicate a need for change.

God is saying, loud and clear, that if we intend to live throughout eternity—if we intend to live for Him in this world—we need to change. If we don't, we will have massive heart failure and die a spiritual death. This is definitely a matter of the heart.

Proverbs 4:23 says, "Keep and guard your heart with all vigilance and above all that you guard, for out of it flow the springs of life." We must be vigilant, constantly examining our own hearts. Otherwise, we will continue to be the "great pretenders." One day the Lord may say to us, "I never knew you; depart from Me, you who act wickedly [disregarding My commands]" (Matt. 7:23).

Heed this warning to care diligently for your new heart:

> Examine and test and evaluate your own selves to see
> whether you are holding to your faith and showing the
> proper fruits of it. Test and prove yourselves [not Christ].
> Do you not yourselves realize and know [thoroughly by
> an ever-increasing experience] that Jesus Christ is in
> you—unless you are [counterfeits] disapproved on trial
> and rejected? But I hope you will recognize and know
> that we are not disapproved on trial and rejected. But
> I pray to God that you may do nothing wrong, not in
> order that we [our teaching] may appear to be approved,
> but that you may continue doing right....
>
> And this we also pray for: your all-round
> strengthening and perfecting of soul. So I write these
> things while I am absent from you, that when I come
> to you, I may not have to deal sharply in my use of the
> authority which the Lord has given me [to be employed,
> however] for building [you] up and not for tearing [you]
> down.
>
> Finally, brethren, farewell (rejoice)! Be strengthened
> (perfected, completed, made what you ought to be); be
> encouraged and consoled and comforted; be of the same
> [agreeable] mind one with another; live in peace, and
> [then] the God of love [Who is the Source of affection,
> goodwill, love, and benevolence toward men] and the
> Author and Promoter of peace will be with you.
>
> —2 Corinthians 13:5–7, 9–11

Memory Verse

*Keep and guard your heart with all vigilance and above all
that you guard, for out of it flow the springs of life.*
—Proverbs 4:23

Heart to Heart

From the depths of your heart, write a prayer to the Giver of your new heart, asking Him to guard you from backsliding:

Dear Father in heaven,

_____

_____

_____

_____

_____

In Jesus' name, amen.

 HEART*BEAT*HEART*BEAT*HEART*BEAT*

Pursue God with your whole heart; if you persist in sin instead, you may lose your new heart.

CHAPTER 11

Prayer Keys

WE HAVE EXAMINED the depths of the heart and mind. Now it's time to put what we know into practice. It's time to take the keys of God's Word and, from the deep chambers of our new hearts, unshackle our minds.

Blessed (happy, fortunate, prosperous, and enviable) is the man who walks and lives not in the counsel of the ungodly [following their advice, their plans and purposes], nor stands [submissive and inactive] in the path where sinners walk, nor sits down [to relax and rest] where the scornful [and the mockers] gather. But his delight and desire are in the law of the Lord, and on His law (the precepts, the instructions, the teachings of God) he habitually meditates (ponders and studies) by day and by night. And he shall be like a tree firmly planted [and tended] by the streams of water, ready to bring forth its fruit in its season; its leaf also shall not fade or wither; and everything he does shall prosper [come to maturity].

—PSALM 1:1–3

It takes about twenty-one days to establish a new habit in your mind. So why don't you challenge yourself—for the next twenty-one days—to study and ponder the Word of God? You will get results.

For the Word that God speaks is alive and full of power [making it active, operative, energizing, and effective]; it is sharper than any two-edged sword, penetrating to the dividing line of the breath of life (soul) and [the immortal] spirit, and of joints and marrow [of the deepest parts of our nature], exposing and sifting and analyzing and judging the very thoughts and purposes of the heart.

—HEBREWS 4:12

THE COUNSEL OF GOD'S WORD

As you seek God in prayer, the Holy Spirit will begin to lead you into the counsel of God's Word. When you hear the voice of God in prayer, He will either speak to you through His Word (using His Word) or by speaking in harmony with what He has already revealed. The more you seek God, the deeper His counsel will become, and the more "secrets" He will reveal. You will gain more and more understanding. (See James 1:5–8.)

The understanding (wisdom) that comes from God "is first of all pure (undefiled); then it is peace-loving, courteous (considerate, gentle). [It is willing to] yield to reason, full of compassion and good fruits; it is wholehearted and straightforward, impartial and unfeigned (free from doubts, wavering, and insincerity)" (James 3:17).

Once you have gained the victory of the new heart, you can consistently receive and respond to the undefiled wisdom of our Father. He can trust you with His secrets. But if you are living in sin, the only thing that God will likely tell you is to repent. Once you have repented from habitual sin, you can then receive the deeper meaning of His heavenly counsel.

As you go deeper in God, He will begin to lead you in everything you do. He will give you intercessory assignments and tell you what to pray according to His Word. He will lead you to be silent or to dance and sing before Him. The most important thing is to do what He leads you to do and to remember what He has already said.

If you do not have one already, it is time to start keeping a prayer journal. Make sure that you write the day, date, and time (and sometimes even the place) when God speaks to you. Write the scriptures that He reveals to you. Sometimes He will give you a verse that describes a problem. When this happens, ask Him to reveal how you can intercede for His solution.

If any of you is deficient in wisdom, let him ask of the giving God [Who gives] to everyone liberally and ungrudgingly, without reproaching or faultfinding, and it will be given him.

—JAMES 1:5

The Wisdom of God

We can possess enough head knowledge to get a PhD or enough life experience to fill a book, but if we lack wisdom, we won't know how to apply anything we have learned.

1.   We read in James 1:5 that God gives wisdom generously. According to this passage, what do we have to *do* to be the recipient of His wisdom?

_____

2.   List several of the qualities of God's wisdom that appear in James 3:17.

_____

_____

_____

3.   In the following Scripture verses, who requested wisdom from God?

1 Kings 3:9   _____

Psalm 51:6   _____

Daniel 1:17 (4 names)   _____

4. One way we can grasp the high importance of gaining God's wisdom is to count the number of times the word is used in the Bible. Read the second chapter of 1 Corinthians. How many times do you see the word *wisdom*? (Your answer will depend on which version you use.) _____

5. Have you asked God for His wisdom today? _____

PRINCIPLES OF PRAYER AND INTERCESSION

Before you can begin to pray effectively, you need to understand exactly what prayer is. First, prayer is *praise* and *petition.* You enter God's presence through your praises, because thanking God proves your faith in Him to perform His Word.

> *Do not fret or have any anxiety about anything, but in every circumstance and in everything, by prayer and petition (definite requests), with thanksgiving, continue to make your wants known to God. And God's peace [shall be yours, that tranquil state of soul assured of its salvation through Christ, and so fearing nothing from God and being content with its earthly lot of whatever sort that is, that peace] which transcends all understanding shall garrison and mount guard over your hearts and minds in Christ Jesus.*
>
> —PHILIPPIANS 4:6–7

There is also an intensified prayer of *consecration* where you press into God with a need to know or to do God's will. (See Matthew 26:39.) Another type of prayer is the prayer of *faith,* or an urgent request for God to intervene in a situation that usually requires an immediate answer. (See James 5:15.) The prayer of *agreement* is joining your faith with two or three others before God. (See Matthew 18:19–20.) *Intercession* is when you pray and believe for someone else. (See Isaiah 59:16.)

According to Matthew 7:7–8, there are also levels (or increasing intensities) of prayer: "Keep on asking and it will be given you; keep on seeking and you will find; keep on knocking [reverently] and [the door] will be opened to you. For everyone who keeps on asking receives; and he who keeps on seeking finds; and to him who keeps on knocking, [the door] will be opened." The kingdom of God is like "something precious buried in a field" (Matt. 13:44). Sometimes we have to dig deeper, wait longer, and press in harder to get the full revelation.

Simply put, to *ask* is to petition God for your needs or to intercede for the needs of others. To *seek* means to ask God for deeper wisdom and, at the same time, to search the Word for deeper insight. Seeking can also mean that you study other resources or look more deeply into the things around you. It can also mean that you receive godly counsel in order to get a full understanding of what God is saying.

Knocking is pressing in further through persistent prayer, fasting, and obedience to God's revealed and written Word. Fasting from food makes your prayers extremely powerful because the devil will not be able to tempt you (because you have already rejected one of the most likely areas of temptation that he can throw in your direction).

GETTING TO THE HEART OF PRAYER

Obviously, prayer is not what it needs to be in the body of Christ, because we are operating from wicked, deceived hearts (Jer. 17:9). Prayer will be restored as we obey our new hearts and renew our

Ask, Seek, Knock

In Luke 11:9–13, Jesus is quoted as saying the same words also recorded in Matthew 7:7–8. He promises that *everyone* who asks will receive, *all* who seek will find, and to *anyone* who knocks, the door will be opened. The key is *doing* it!

1. The words about asking, seeking, and knocking come immediately after the parable about the man who knocked on his friend's door late at night to ask for some bread (v. 8). What word would you use to describe the particular personal trait Jesus is trying to emphasize in verses 8–9?

2. What kind of a contrast or comparison does Jesus portray in verses 11–13 of this chapter?

3. What is the ultimate gift that Jesus gives us (v. 13)?

4. What must you do to receive the Holy Spirit?

old, stubborn minds. Today, in this season and final hour of the church, prayer will be the final test of any genuine believer or work for God.

Dwell in Me, and I will dwell in you. [Live in Me, and I will live in you.] Just as no branch can bear fruit of itself without abiding in (being vitally united to) the vine, neither can you bear fruit unless you abide in Me. I am the Vine; you are the branches. Whoever lives in Me and I in him bears much (abundant) fruit. However, apart from Me [cut off from vital union with Me] you

Getting Personal

To be honest, I used to be a "prayer bum," like many other Christians. You know what I mean. I gave lip service to the importance of prayer, but I really didn't give much time to it. I thought of it as a duty and a chore.

But when I got filled with the Holy Spirit, it was like I developed an instant "heart for prayer." I just wanted to talk with the Lord about everything. I didn't want to do things without Him. Now prayer is like breathing, it's so natural. I pray about everything.

I sit down and have a special time of prayer alone each day, and I also pray as I take care of my daily affairs. Sometimes I'm asking God for things, sometimes I'm listening, and sometimes I'm just being grateful. Just this morning as I happened to see the sun came up over the tops of the buildings across the street, my heart just jumped with joy, and I said, "I love You, Lord!" I never used to do things like that before!

—A. J.

> *can do nothing. If a person does not dwell in Me, he is thrown out like a [broken-off] branch, and withers; such branches are gathered up and thrown into the fire, and they are burned. If you live in Me [abide vitally united to Me] and My words remain in you and continue to live in your hearts, ask whatever you will, and it shall be done for you.*
>
> —John 15:4–7

Prayer is our vital connection to God through the vehicle of our new hearts. If we do not pray, we will not have the life of Christ within us. We will be unproductive and, even worse, could be thrown out like a "broken-off branch" (John 15:6).

THE PRACTICE OF PRAYER

(This has been adapted from a powerful, in-depth teaching called "The Power of Positive Prayer" in Matthew Ashimolowo's special edition Bible.[1])

---

1. Matthew Ashimolowo Media Ministries, London, England. Web site: www.kicc.org.uk

1. Start each day loving God and people. This means your relationship with God is good, and that as far as you are able, your relationships with family members, friends, co-workers, and others are in line with the Word.

2. Start each day communing with God through Bible study and prayer.

3. Thank God, praise Him for answering your prayer, and worship Him for who He is.

4. Repent, asking God to forgive you and to cleanse your heart from every sin, known and unknown.

5. Thank God for your spiritual armor, as listed in Ephesians 6:10–18.

6. Surrender yourself to the Holy Spirit so He can pray through you, according to Romans 8:26–27.

7. Be ready to obey the Holy Spirit's leading to petition (for your needs) or to intercede (for others); declare God's Word; lie still; or do whatever God leads you to do.

8. Ask God to build a hedge of protection around your life, family, and all others who are praying with you against the enemy's devices.

9. Ask God to rebuke Satan and all his servants.

10. Take authority over the enemy's work and his attempts to attack your new heart (spirit), your mind (emotions, logic, and decision making), and your body.

11. Repeat these steps until you know that you have broken through in the spirit realm and that God is leading you in prayer and intercession.

A Few Prayer Keys for the Heart

You can use these scriptures as you seek God in prayer daily, learning to embrace your new heart. I have chosen scriptures that can be used as a personal expression of prayer. I have used the Hebrew word *selah* from the Psalms, to remind you to linger and meditate prayerfully on the verse or verses. (My Amplified Bible attaches the phrase *pause, and calmly think of that* to the word *selah.*) You can use the blank lines for writing down insights and personal applications.

> *Create in me a clean heart, O God, and renew a right, persevering, and steadfast spirit within me. . . . Let the words of my mouth and the meditation of my heart be acceptable in Your sight, O Lord, my [firm, impenetrable] Rock and my Redeemer.*
>
> —PSALM 51:10; 19:14

Selah

_____

_____

> *Search me [thoroughly], O God, and know my heart! Try me and know my thoughts! And see if there is any wicked or hurtful way in me, and lead me in the way everlasting.*
>
> —PSALM 139:23–24

Selah

_____

_____

> *Teach me Your way, O Lord, that I may walk and live in Your truth; direct and unite my heart [solely, reverently] to fear and honor Your name.*
>
> —PSALM 86:11

Selah

_____

_____

I delight to do Your will, O my God; yes, Your law is within my heart.
—PSALM 40:8

Selah

_____

_____

A Few Prayer Keys for the Mind

Use the following scriptures to help you think about God's purposes for your mind. "Pause and calmly think about" each one (*selah*).

For who has known or understood the mind (the counsels and purposes) of the Lord so as to guide and instruct Him and give Him knowledge? But we have the mind of Christ (the Messiah) and do hold the thoughts (feelings and purposes) of His heart.
—1 CORINTHIANS 2:16

Selah

_____

_____

And be not conformed to this world: but be ye transformed by the renewing of your mind, that ye may prove what is that good, and acceptable, and perfect, will of God.
—ROMANS 12:2, KJV

Selah

_____

_____

And be constantly renewed in the spirit of your mind [having a fresh mental and spiritual attitude], and put on the new nature (the regenerate self) created in God's image, [Godlike] in true righteousness and holiness.

—EPHESIANS 4:23–24

Selah

You will guard him and keep him in perfect and constant peace whose mind [both its inclination and its character] is stayed on You, because he commits himself to You, leans on You, and hopes confidently in You.

—ISAIAH 26:3

Selah

I will imprint My laws upon their minds, even upon their innermost thoughts and understanding, and engrave them upon their hearts; and I will be their God, and they shall be My people.

—HEBREWS 8:10

Selah

For God did not give us a spirit of timidity (of cowardice, of craven and cringing and fawning fear), but [He has given us a spirit] of power and of love and of calm and well-balanced mind and discipline and self-control.

—2 TIMOTHY 1:7

Selah

> *So brace up your minds; be sober (circumspect, morally alert); set your hope wholly and unchangeably on the grace (divine favor) that is coming to you when Jesus Christ (the Messiah) is revealed.*
>
> —1 PETER 1:13
>
> *Selah*

Nothing is more important than the matters of the heart.

Therefore also now, says the Lord, turn and keep on coming to Me with all your heart, with fasting, with weeping, and with mourning [until every hindrance is removed and the broken fellowship is restored]. Rend your hearts and not your garments and return to the Lord, your God, for He is gracious and merciful, slow to anger and abounding in loving-kindness; and He revokes His sentence of evil [when His conditions are met].

—JOEL 2:12–13

Memory Verse

You will guard him and keep him in perfect and constant peace whose mind [both its inclination and its character] is stayed on You, because he commits himself to You, leans on You, and hopes confidently in You.

—ISAIAH 26:3

Heart to Heart

U se the Power of Positive Prayer points to guide your prayer to God:

Dear God,

_____

_____

_____

_____

_____

_____

_____ .

H E A R T B E A T H E A R T B E A T H E A R T B E A T

Prayer is our vital connection to God through the vehicle of our new hearts.

CHAPTER 12

Living With Your New Heart

IF YOU HAVE read this far through this book, I hope that by now you have asked God for the new heart. I'm going to assume you have done it. With your new heart, your life will explode with good things. It will be abundant! (See the promise in John 10:10.)

If you had just had a physical heart transplant, it would be important for you to take care of your new heart. This chapter is about taking good care of your new heart from God, and we will review what we have learned already.

We have learned that having Jesus' heart beating in our chests will cause us to begin to look something like Him. We start to walk and talk like Jesus, move like He does, and express His godly reactions. This "family resemblance" includes a lot more than just "nice" behavior and attendance at church functions. It's a total *transformation*.

> Now the Lord is the Spirit, and where the Spirit of the Lord is, there is liberty (emancipation from bondage, freedom). And all of us, as with unveiled face, [because we] continued to behold [in the Word of God] as in a mirror the glory of the Lord, are constantly being transfigured into His very own image in ever increasing splendor and from one degree of glory to another; [for this comes] from the Lord [Who is] the Spirit.
> —2 CORINTHIANS 3:17–18

SOMETHING IS DIFFERENT

As your new heart keeps beating steadily, day and night, sending the cleansing blood of Jesus throughout your whole being, are you noticing changes? Is your mind getting the message? Are you different? Or are you experiencing some problems? Are you having some symptoms of heart rejection? (That would be bad news, but it can be reversed. Don't ignore any symptoms of heart rejection!)

It's time for a checkup with your Cardiologist (God). He will run some tests and talk to you about the results. He wants to see how you are doing with your transplanted heart. He does not want any of His patients to experience heart rejection.

Repent and turn from all your transgressions, lest iniquity be your ruin and so shall they not be a stumbling block to you. Cast away from you all your transgressions by which you have transgressed against Me, and make you a new mind and heart and a new spirit.... Therefore turn (be converted) and live!

—EZEKIEL 18:30–32

Many Are Called, Few Are Chosen

Jesus said, "Many are called (invited and summoned), but few are chosen" (Matt. 22:14). Another way of saying this might be, "Many people hear the gospel message, but relatively few of them respond to it by asking for a new heart with which to live out their call."

1.   Does everyone who has been "called" realize it? _____

Why or why not?

_____

_____

2. Does God force us to say *yes* to His call? _____

3. What are some distinguishing features of someone who has responded to God's invitation to become one of the "chosen"?

_____

_____

_____

4. The Greek word for church, *ekklesia,* means "called-out ones." In your church body, do you see people who exhibit the distinguishing features from your list in question #3 above? Reflect on whether or not you are part of a congregation of people who have heard and heeded God's call.

_____

_____

_____

5. List a few reasons you know you are walking as a "chosen" one. (Think also of how you know you have the new heart.)

_____

_____

_____

Questions to think about:

• Why is Jesus not more "inclusive"?

• Why does He insist on such a high standard, such a "narrow way"? (See Matthew 7:14.)

• Wouldn't you think He would want to lower His standards so He could have more people in His kingdom?

• If He lowered His standards, how would this change the nature or quality of the kingdom of God?

THE CHECKUP

You have kept your doctor's appointment, and now you are sitting on the examining table dressed in one of those skimpy little gowns. The doctor enters the room.

"Good afternoon," he says, briskly but warmly. "How's my favorite transplant patient?"

"I'm feeling pretty good."

"I'm glad to hear that. What improvements have you noticed since your last checkup?"

"Well, I sure have more energy than I used to. I feel younger. I'm keeping up with my exercises, and I know I'm regaining strength. In fact, I'm probably going to become stronger than I was before."

"I know you will."

"Also, I'm warmer. It's like my circulation is working now. When I touch someone, they don't say, 'Oh, your hand is so cold!'"

"I can tell by looking at you that your circulation is 100 percent better."

"And my mental and emotional health is much improved. The other day, my son fell off some steps and broke his wrist. That might not seem like a big deal to others, but in the past it would have been hard for me to react right, especially because it happened just as I was leaving for work. (Yes, I'm back to work, too. I'm putting in almost a full workday now.) When my son fell, I was already late to work, which could have made me more anxious than I should be—and even angry. But I just took it in stride and attended to him. Of course, it meant I had to miss some work, but they were OK with that. Not only could I give comfort to my little boy, but also I could see a difference in the way I did things. It was like I could think straighter and make decisions better. I could figure out my moves—how to get to the ER, how to call work and what to say, and how to get him the help he needed. I'm really doing a lot better since getting the new heart."

The doctor, looking pleased at your report, starts to listen to your new heart with his stethoscope…

Before and After

Briefly note some differences you have noticed in yourself "Before the New Heart" and "After the New Heart." You may not have something to write for every category. Think of your responses as part of your "heart checkup."

1. *My relationships.* What are they like—family, spouse, children, friends, co-workers?

Before the New Heart:

_____

_____

After the New Heart:

_____

_____

2. *My job.* What is the state of my work life? Am I doing "all for the honor and glory of God" (1 Cor. 10:31) and "rendering service readily with goodwill, as to the Lord and not to men" (Eph. 6:7)?

Before the New Heart:

_____

_____

After the New Heart:

_____

_____

3. *My possessions.* Do I possess too much stuff or too little? Do I own it, or does it own me?

Before the New Heart:

_____

_____

After the New Heart:

_____

_____

4. *My money.* Do I have enough money or too little? Am I overspending? Am I being honest in my finances?

Before the New Heart:

_____

_____

After the New Heart:

_____

_____

5. *My leisure time.* Am I making good choices about my "down time"? Am I considerate of others? Am I selfish?

Before the New Heart:

_____

_____

After the New Heart:

_____

_____

6. *Serving others.* Am I doing things for other people? Do I have a good attitude about helping others?

Before the New Heart:

_____

_____

After the New Heart:

_____

_____

7. *God.* Do I have an ongoing, *daily* relationship with God? Do I pray often? Do I hear from Him? Do I read the Bible?

Before the New Heart:

_____

_____

After the New Heart:

_____

_____

8. *My speech.* Am I ashamed of anything I have said? Am I blessing others with my words?

Before the New Heart:

_____

_____

After the New Heart:

_____

_____

9. *My home.* Wherever I am in charge of my home environment, is my household serving God? Am I hesitant to let people see anything in my home?

Before the New Heart:

_____

_____

After the New Heart:

_____

_____

10. *My marriage and family.* [If you are married] Am I loving my spouse the way the Lord has instructed? [If you have children] Am I raising them well? (See Ephesians 5.)

Before the New Heart:

_____

_____

After the New Heart:

_____

_____

Read through the list again, and ask yourself two questions about each item on the list:

1.   Am I willing to obey Jesus in this area—regardless of what He tells me to do?

2.   Am I able to thank God for whatever might happen in this area?

Examine and test and evaluate your own selves to see whether you are holding to your faith and showing the proper fruits of it. Test and prove yourselves [not Christ]. Do you not yourselves realize and know [thoroughly by an ever-increasing experience] that Jesus Christ is in you—unless you are [counterfeits] disapproved on trial and rejected?

—2 CORINTHIANS 13:5

"You Are Here"

You have seen those big maps posted in public places with "You Are Here" to show you where you are. With the help of the map, you can get to your destination. Where are you on the map of the New Heart?

☐ At the entrance—just looking in

☐ Inside, but still able to see back through the outside door to my Old Heart life

☐ Inside, looking around and getting acclimated to this new place

☐ Inside already for a long time, getting quite familiar with everything

☐ Inside for a very long time, and so comfortable in the New Heart that it feels like home

STATE OF SURRENDER

To continue your checkup, let's examine your state of surrender to the new heart the Lord has given you. Have you embraced your new heart? How much have you given up control of your life so that Jesus, who died to save you from futility, can have you for Himself?

Are you working out your own salvation "with reverence and awe and trembling" (Phil. 2:12)? Paul wrote those words to the

Philippians, who had been born again like you and me. He wanted them to know that there was *work* ahead and that they could not experience full salvation unless they cooperated with that work. What does the work consist of?

When we looked at the parable of the sower (Matt. 13; Mark 4; Luke 8), we saw that regardless of the kind of soil the seeds fell on, the growth process happened the same way—the individual seeds had to burst through their hard outer coatings. The little sprouts began to grow only after there was a kind of death. The seed didn't exist anymore. It had to die in order to birth a plant.

We don't always like the idea, but it is true that our spiritual growth does not occur without brokenness and death to our old self. Our seed must surrender. After our outer "husk" has split open and fallen off, God will bring forth our true nature. Then our life will start to grow as it was meant to. It's not really all that complicated!

Over the course of our lifetimes, we will re-surrender many times as we grow. Here are some areas of surrender that we need to revisit from time to time.

Forgiveness

Sometimes we will run into invisible roadblocks. Our new hearts are beating along normally, and all of a sudden they start beating double-time. Often, our "irregular heartbeat" is because we need to forgive somebody.

"I Forgive You"

1. Is there someone you have tried to forgive, but you find that the person's account of wrongs keeps being reopened in your mind?

2.   What did this person do to you? (Or what do you *perceive* that this person did to you? Your spiritual well-being depends on turning over your negative reactions to Him.)

_____

_____

3.   Is the person still doing it to you?

4.   Do you somehow feel that you can't forgive the person because the wrongdoing continues? Or do you feel, perhaps, that you should maintain your unforgiveness to make a statement about the severity of the wrong?

_____

5.   What did the person take away from you (possessions, reputation, safety, respect, etc.)?

_____

_____

6.   How do you feel about what happened (angry, afraid, vindictive, helpless, rejected, etc.)?

_____

_____

7.   "Be gentle and forbearing with one another and, if one has a difference (a grievance or complaint) against another, readily pardoning each other; even as the Lord has [freely] forgiven you, so must you also [forgive]" (Col. 3:13). On the lines below, put this verse into your own words, substituting the name(s) of the person or people you need to forgive. Forgiving them and "forbearing with" them does not mean you need to be physically or emotionally close to them, which could be dangerous to you.

_____

_____

You don't need to "feel forgiving" in order to obey God's command to forgive. Ask Him to help you do it. Then, as many times as you feel you need to do so, you can pray the following prayer:

> *Dear Lord,*
>   *Even though this is difficult to do, I want to obey Your command to forgive others just as You have forgiven me. I know that You see what happened and that You are just in all that You do. Trusting that You will take care of seeing justice done, I want to hand over what this person did to me. Please take care of my heart, which has been wounded. If my thoughts return to this situation, please help me to turn them over to You, trusting that You have taken this matter over and that I don't have to maintain my grievance. Help me to develop an attitude of forgiveness and a heart that is so full of Your love that it covers a multitude of wrongs.*
>   *In Jesus' name and because of His sacrifice, amen.*

Double-mindedness

"Wash your hands, you sinners, and purify your hearts, you double-minded" (James 4:8, NIV). Notice the connection between the heart and the mind. If you are double-*minded*, the cure is achieving purity of *heart*. Maintaining your purity of heart is like insurance against double-mindedness.

You know you are dealing with double-mindedness when you say, "Well, part of me wants to do this thing, and part of me doesn't," or simply when you let the voice of your old nature prevail over the messages from your new heart. It's like having two minds. Even though one side of your will wants what is right, the other side yields to what is wrong, such as jealousy or covetousness or some other sinful behavior.

Elijah came near to all the people and said, How long will you halt and limp between two opinions? If the Lord is God, follow Him! But if Baal, then follow him.

—1 KINGS 18:21

Strongholds

Strongholds are sinful structures that persist in our lives. Strongholds are like pockets of resistance to the lordship of Jesus— habits, concepts, expectations, doctrines, and so forth. These patterns of thought and behavior almost seem to be part of our personalities.

The combination of the new heart and a renewed mind equips us to demolish the strongholds that plague us. Common strongholds include pride, independence, unforgiveness, control/manipulation, fear, and anger/being critical.

Our goal is to have only one Stronghold—the Lord Himself. "The name of the LORD is a strong tower: the righteous runneth into it, and is safe" (Prov. 18:10, KJV).

> For thus says the Lord to the house of Israel: See Me [inquire for and of Me and require Me as you require food], and you shall live!…the Lord is His name—Who causes sudden destruction to flash forth upon the strong so that destruction comes upon the fortress.
>
> —AMOS 5:4, 8–9

Healthy habits

Healthy heart habits include regular Bible reading, personal and group prayer, and worship. They help us develop qualities such as trust, love, and obedience, which enable us to reflect God's life,

Time to Uproot

To everything there is a season, and a time for every matter or purpose under heaven: A time to be born and a time to die, a time to plant and a time to pluck up what is planted.

—ECCLESIASTES 3:1–2

There is a time to uproot strongholds, one at a time. (God doesn't want to destroy us by transforming us too fast.)

1. Can you identify a particular stronghold that God may have on the "front burner" of your life right now? (You may not know for sure.)

_____

2. Is there a pattern of troublesome thinking that you can identify because of this stronghold? For example, out of a stronghold of fear, you may behave in a way that seems irrational—being very afraid of dogs, or becoming paralyzed at the thought of speaking into a microphone.

_____

_____

3. If you haven't demolished the stronghold of fear in your life, it won't do you much permanent good to paste fear-busting scriptures all over your bathroom mirror or even to get delivered from an evil spirit of fear. The stronghold will just sit there like an immovable object, and soon you will find your mind filled with fears again. What can you do? You can lay siege to a stronghold that God has shown you. "Whatever you bind on earth will be bound in heaven, and whatever you loose on earth will be loosed in heaven" (Matt. 16:19; 18:18, NIV).

> *In the strong name of Jesus, I attack the stronghold of _____*
> *_____ and bring it down. I loose myself from ungodly patterns of*
> *_____ _____. Without hesitation, I bind my will to the*
> *will of Christ, and I bind my mind and my heart to Jesus, the Lord*
> *of Life.*

You can make this prayer your own as you learn more about how God wants to set you free.

to pray according to His will, and to live happy, long lives. Let's look at a few of these "heart healthy" practices:

Daily prayer. Prayer is a two-way conversation with God. It is your lifeline. Try to set aside some time every single day to talk one-on-one with the One who is the source of your life and all wisdom. In chapter eleven, we took a look at prayer. Use any "prayer keys" that match your personality and your lifestyle.

Fasting. I mentioned fasting in chapter eleven in conjunction with prayer. Fasting is a powerful weapon! You might not feel very powerful when you are hungry, but the enemy sees and trembles. Fasting can include giving up something besides food, such as watching TV or drinking soda.

Serving others. "For we do not preach ourselves, but Jesus Christ as Lord, and ourselves as your servants for Jesus' sake" (2 Cor. 4:5, NIV). We do not preach a "self-serve" gospel. The body of Christ is meant to function as a team of people who are gifted to serve each other and to reach out to others outside the body.

Worship. When all is said and done, there will still be worship. While we are living here in the earth realm, we are "tuning up" in preparation for an eternity of worship in heaven. Some worship is solo, and some is like a choir. And although music is wonderful, it is not all music! You can do almost anything as an act of worship.

Fellowship. Yes, spending time with your brothers and sisters in Christ is good for your heart! Do not neglect getting together with others, whether for work or for fun. (See Hebrews 10:24–25.)

Study. There is always something more to learn about the Word and about God. He shows us many things by revelation, and He prefers to teach us as we take time to listen to good teaching, read good books (especially the Word), and use our renewed minds to *think* about His kingdom.

Heart Habits

1.   In which of the heart habits above am I the strongest? _____

In which am I the weakest? _____

What steps can I take to improve? (Remember to ask Him to help you.)

_____

_____

2.   Write down one or two ways in which you exercise the heart habits above. For example, after "Study," you could write "doing this study guide."

•   Daily prayer   _____

•   Fasting   _____

•   Serving others   _____

•   Worship   _____

•   Fellowship   _____

•   Study   _____

3.   Read aloud 2 Peter 1:5–8 from the Amplified Bible. (It has been reformatted with bullets to help you grasp the significance of each step.)

•   "For this very reason, adding your diligence [to the divine promises], employ every effort in exercising your faith to develop virtue (excellence, resolution, Christian energy),

•   "...and in [exercising] virtue [develop] knowledge (intelligence),

•   "...and in [exercising] knowledge [develop] self-control;

•   "...and in [exercising] self-control [develop] steadfastness (patience, endurance),

•   "...and in [exercising] steadfastness [develop] godliness (piety),

•   "...and in [exercising] godliness [develop] brotherly affection,

•   "...and in [exercising] brotherly affection [develop] Christian love.

- "For as these qualities are yours and increasingly abound in you, they will keep [you] from being idle or unfruitful unto the [full personal] knowledge of our Lord Jesus Christ (the Messiah, the Anointed One)."

YOU TAKE IT FROM HERE!

Our journey from old heart to new is now complete. Your personal journey is eternal, and it will get better and better. Taking Paul's advice below, run with it!

As you have therefore received Christ, [even] Jesus the Lord, [so] walk (regulate your lives and conduct yourselves) in union with and conformity to Him. Have the roots [of your being] firmly and deeply planted [in Him, fixed and founded in Him], being continually built up in Him, becoming increasingly more confirmed and established in the faith, just as you were taught, and abounding and overflowing in it with thanksgiving.

See to it that no one carries you off as spoil or makes you yourselves captive by his so-called philosophy and intellectualism and vain deceit (idle fancies and plain nonsense), following human tradition (men's ideas of the material rather than the spiritual world), just crude notions following the rudimentary and elemental teachings of the universe and disregarding [the teachings of] Christ (the Messiah).

For in Him the whole fullness of Deity (the Godhead) continues to dwell in bodily form [giving complete expression of the divine nature]. And you are in Him, made full and having come to fullness of life [in Christ you too are filled with the Godhead—Father,

Son and Holy Spirit—and reach full spiritual stature].
And He is the Head of all rule and authority [of every
angelic principality and power].

—Colossians 2:6–10

Memory Verse	*Trust in him at all times, O people; pour out your hearts to him,* *for God is our refuge.*
	—Psalm 62:8, NIV

Heart to Heart

What do you want to say to the Lord of your new heart? Pour out your heart to Him, as Psalm 62:8 tells us:

_____

_____

_____

_____

_____

_____

 H E A R T ᴮ E A T H E A R T ᴮ E A T H E A R T ᴮ E A T

Take care of your new heart—
your spiritual life depends on it.

LEARN HOW HIS WORDS CAN CHANGE YOUR LIFE!

We pray that these powerful words have impacted your life and that each day will bring about a transformation in your heart.

Now you can dig a little deeper and explore the heart/mind connection and see why this key to intimacy with God is so vital to a healthy, satisfying, and effective life.

$13.99 / 0-88419-832-4

More than 500,000 copies sold! CHARISMA HOUSE PUBLISHING

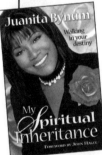

All Christians have a spiritual inheritance, but many aren't aware of it. Juanita Bynum takes you right to the core issue, and she minces no words as she describes how to move into the full portion of God's inheritance for us.

$19.99 / 1-59185-412-1

This companion resource to *My Spiritual Inheritance* contains 15 chapters with Scripture verses and opportunities to track your progress—and even share it with others.

$11.99 / 1-59185-634-5

Call 1-800-599-5750 to order!
Visit our Web site at charismahouse.com
and save even more.

Charisma HOUSE
A STRANG COMPANY
Everything good starts here!

4217-2

Strang Communications, the publisher of both Charisma House and *Charisma* magazine, wants to give you 3 FREE ISSUES to our award-winning magazine.

Since its inception in 1975, *Charisma* magazine has helped thousands of Christians stay connected with what God is doing worldwide.

Within its pages you will discover in-depth reports and the latest news from a Christian perspective, biblical health tips, global events in the body of Christ, personality profiles, and so much more. Join the family of *Charisma* readers who enjoy feeding their spirit each month with miracle-filled testimonies and inspiring articles that bring clarity, provoke prayer, and demand answers.

To claim your **3 free issues** of *Charisma,* send your name and address to: Charisma 3 Free Issue Offer, 600 Rinehart Road, Lake Mary, FL 32746. Or you may call 1-800-829-3346 and ask for Offer # 93FREE. This offer is only valid in the USA.

www.charismamag.com

3581